A Veiled Gazelle

Books by Idries Shah

Sufi Studies and Middle Eastern Literature
The Sufis
Caravan of Dreams
The Way of the Sufi
Tales of the Dervishes: *Teaching-stories Over a
Thousand Years*
Sufi Thought and Action

**Traditional Psychology,
Teaching Encounters and Narratives**
Thinkers of the East: *Studies in Experientialism*
Wisdom of the Idiots
The Dermis Probe
Learning How to Learn: *Psychology and Spirituality
in the Sufi Way*
Knowing How to Know
The Magic Monastery: *Analogical and Action Philosophy*
Seeker After Truth
Observations
Evenings with Idries Shah
The Commanding Self

University Lectures
A Perfumed Scorpion (Institute for the Study of
Human Knowledge and California University)
Special Problems in the Study of Sufi Ideas
(Sussex University)
The Elephant in the Dark: *Christianity,
Islam and the Sufis* (Geneva University)
Neglected Aspects of Sufi Study: *Beginning to Begin*
(The New School for Social Research)
Letters and Lectures of Idries Shah

.

Current and Traditional Ideas
Reflections
The Book of the Book
A Veiled Gazelle: *Seeing How to See*
Special Illumination: *The Sufi Use of Humour*

The Mulla Nasrudin Corpus
The Pleasantries of the Incredible Mulla Nasrudin
The Subtleties of the Inimitable Mulla Nasrudin
The Exploits of the Incomparable Mulla Nasrudin
The World of Nasrudin

Travel and Exploration
Destination Mecca

Studies in Minority Beliefs
The Secret Lore of Magic
Oriental Magic

Selected Folktales and Their Background
World Tales

A Novel
Kara Kush

Sociological Works
Darkest England
The Natives Are Restless
The Englishman's Handbook

Translated by Idries Shah
The Hundred Tales of Wisdom (Aflaki's *Munaqib*)

A VEILED GAZELLE

A VEILED GAZELLE
'Seeing how to See'

by

Idries Shah

'Among the wondrous things
is a Veiled Gazelle...'
Ibn Arabi

ISF PUBLISHING

Contents

Introduction

And among the wondrous things is a
*   veiled gazelle:*
A Divine Subtlety, veiled by a state of
*   the Self,*
Referring to the States of those who
*   know. Unable to explain their*
*   perceptions to others, they can only*
*   indicate them to whoever has started*
*   to feel something similar...*
                    Muhiyuddin ibn Arabi,
                    The Interpreter of Desires

THE VEILED GAZELLES, or shrouded deer
(*Dhabiyun mubarqa'un*) referred to by Ibn Arabi
are the perceptions and experiences indicated by
those who have them to those who have some
inkling of them. 'Veiling' in Sufi parlance indicates
the action of the subjective or 'commanding' self,
which partly through indoctrination and partly
through base aspirations prevents higher vision.

Sufi poetry, literature, tales and activities are the instruments which, when employed with insight and prescription rather than automatically or obsessively, help in the relationship between Sufi and pupil, towards the removal of the veils.

Idries Shah

Master of the Option

THREE YOUNG MEN, each having heard of the great sanctity and wonders wrought by the Sufi master Kilidi, chanced to meet on their way to his dwelling-place. Journeying together, they discussed what they knew of the Path and its difficulties.

'Sincerity towards your teacher is essential,' said the first youth, 'and I shall concentrate upon that, if I am accepted as a student, to exclude my own baser selfishness.'

'Sincerity,' said the second, 'of course means complete obedience, even when provoked to rebel. And I certainly shall abide by that. But obedience also means to avoid hypocrisy – desiring inwardly to disobey – and includes generosity without pride. That I will attempt.'

'Sincerity, avoiding base selfishness, obedience, detachment from hypocrisy, generosity,' said the third, 'these are essentials. But I have heard it said that if the disciple tries to graft these on top of his unaltered self, they merely become mechanical, mimes, even hiding objectionable characteristics which wait to manifest themselves. Surely the real disciple is he who is not just doing the opposite of what he feels is bad, nor carrying on a charade of "goodness". They say that he is a Seeker of Truth who is master of the option, to do good or to do what has to be done.'

They all arrived, eventually, at the Sufi's house, and were allowed to attend some of his lectures and to take part in various spiritually strengthening exercises.

One day the Sufi said to them: 'Whether we are at home or on the road, we are all, always on a journey. But to give this illustrative effect I shall now give you the chance of observing and taking part in one such expedition, in a perceptible shape.'

After they had been on the road for some time, the first disciple said to the Sufi: 'Travel is undoubtedly good, but my mind inclines to service, the Sufi station in which one can obtain understanding through working for others and for the Truth.'

The Sufi answered: 'Would you like to establish yourself in a cell at this crossroads, and serve the people, until such time as I call you to further studies?' The young man was delighted to have this opportunity of carrying out a task on his own, and the others left him there to attend to the needs of the wayfarer.

Some time later the second disciple said to the Sufi: 'I yearn to turn back from my self-centredness, so that my Commanding Self shall be able to exercise sincerity. I wish I could pause at this village, and explain some of the respect which I have for you and for the Path to the people here, who plainly have no comprehension of it.'

'If that is your wish, I shall grant it,' said the Sufi. Leaving him there in a state of delight, the Sufi and his remaining disciple moved on.

Some days later, these two came to a place where people were fighting about which of them should have a certain piece of land and farm it, and who should have another. The young man said to the Sufi: 'How strange that they do not see that, by working together, they would all benefit far more: they should pool both their resources and their labour, to achieve prosperity.'

'Now,' said the Sufi, 'you can see that you are the master of the option here. You can see alternatives that others cannot. Your option is to tell them or to pass by silently.'

'I do not want to tell them,' said the youth, 'since they might not listen to me and would probably all turn against me. So nothing would be gained, and I would only be diverted from my goal on the Path.'

'Very well,' said the Sufi, 'I shall intervene.'

He approached the people, and by some means known only to himself, made them give up the land to him. He settled there, and after a few years, when he had taught everyone to

3

share in the labour, he presented the land and its yield to them, and the two started again on their interrupted journey.

They retraced their steps and when they arrived at the place where they had left the second disciple, the third student noticed that this man did not recognise them. Their appearance had changed, through years of work on the land, the effect of the sun, and their change of clothes. They even spoke, through long association with the villagers, in a somewhat different manner.

To the second disciple, therefore, they were merely two villagers. The Sufi approached the second disciple and asked him to tell him something about the Sufi teacher who had left him there some years before.

'Don't you talk to me about him,' said his former disciple; 'for he abandoned me here to make his fame known in the land, giving me to understand that he would return and teach me – and I have had no word of him for several years.'

And, for some reason originating with the Beyond, as soon as he had said these words, a number of villagers appeared and seized him. The newcomers asked their chief why they were acting in this way. 'This man,' said the villagers, 'came here and preached about a great man of the spirit whose disciple he was. We took him in and he became rich and successful in our village. We decided, five minutes ago, that he is a liar and a fraud, and we are taking him away to kill him.' There was nothing that the two could do as the unfortunate man was hauled struggling away, although they tried. 'You see?' said the Sufi. 'I have tried to protect him, but here I am not master of the option.'

They journeyed on, until they came to the place where there sat the first disciple, at the crossroads. He, too, did not recognise them. When they approached, the Sufi asked him where they might find some water to drink. The disciple answered: 'I am thoroughly disillusioned with you travellers. I have been here for years trying to help the people, and all I got was betrayal. People are not worth serving. Even my master, who deserted me three years or more ago, is not prepared to serve *me* by coming back and giving me the teachings to which all men are surely entitled...'

No sooner were these words out of his mouth than a party of soldiers arrived and seized the man for forced labour. 'We thought that you were only a poor ascetic,' said their captain, 'but as we paused to watch you, we noticed by your belligerent air and violent actions as you gesticulated, that you were strong enough to do some service for the State.' In spite of the Sufi and his disciple remonstrating with them, the soldiers carried the first disciple off. 'I am not the master of the option here, as you can see,' said the Sufi to the third disciple.

In this way did Kilidi show the only disciple who had the patience to understand that the understanding of events and their action are interrelated, and that how a person behaves inwardly and outwardly will determine his progress just as much as anything done by anyone else.

He asked the disciple: 'If you were asked what you have learnt, how would you put it?'

The young man said: 'People look at things in isolation, imagining that if they do what they want to do they will surely get what they want. Further, their good brings harvests and their bad brings harvests, and none can stand in the way of one's harvest. And I have learnt that on the path all are entwined: people, places, events and actions. Finally, I have learnt that while someone's bad thoughts and actions may remove all his hopes of progress, there is yet a Merciful dispensation: for have I myself not been allowed to continue learning in spite of my refusal to exercise the option when I was master of it?'

At that moment there was a rushing sound, and the third disciple became aware of the truth of the Greater Understanding; and, as this was happening, the Sufi teacher Kilidi disappeared, never to be seen again.

He walked the remainder of the way to the house of the teacher, where a large number of dervishes were waiting, and as he entered it, he placed Kilidi's prayer-carpet, which he had picked up, on the master's chair. The watching dervishes raised a great shout of welcome, and their leader approached the third disciple.

'Master,' he said, 'we have been waiting here under a vow of secrecy for over three years, since the Great Sheikh Kilidi left us saying that he was returning to the skies, and that whoever should bring back his prayer-carpet would be his successor.'

Now this dervish was heavily veiled with the end of his turban. As he handed over the establishment to the third disciple, now the master, and prepared to go on his own travels, the cloth momentarily moved aside from his features and the new Sufi teacher saw the face of Kilidi, smiling, before him.

Four Friends

ONCE UPON A time there was a Sufi who had decided to take up his abode in a certain city, where he was to establish his school. There were three men there who knew his work, and who had written to him expressing their desire to be of help to him in any way he wished.

Accordingly, he visited them one by one.

The first was one of the best-known scholars of the region, who said to him:

'You are more than welcome, and I would like to be of any service to you and your work, and, of course, I also want to study under you.'

The Sufi thanked him and said: 'I would indeed like to teach you, but first of all we have preparatory work to do: a house cannot be lived in until it is built.'

'Command me,' said the scholar.

The Sufi continued: 'Supposing that I become a person who is much discussed in this city, I would like you to become my critic, using your scholarly capacities, within reasonable limits, to put the logical case against my work, in an adequate and rational manner.'

'This is indeed a strange request,' said the scholar, 'far from the familiar methods of the ordinary thinker. But I have promised to serve you, and I shall attempt to do what you ask.'

The Sufi left him and went to see the second man, who was an influential and literate lawyer, also much respected in the area.

The lawyer also expressed a wish, to be of help and to be a disciple, and the Sufi said:

'I would much like you to study under me; but first I will accept your offer to help in whatever way you can. I ask you to do the following:

'If and when you hear that I am being discussed in this city, you are to defend my name and work, in as reasonable manner as you can, so that I have a logical and cool-headed supporter.'

'I would be glad to act in this capacity,' said the merchant, 'though I certainly did not realise that people of probity were ever in need of arranged support.'

Finally, the Sufi presented himself at the court of the third man, who happened to be the governor of the city. The governor expressed the desire to be a pupil and to be of any possible service to the Sufi, whom he respected so much, and the Sufi thanked him and put this proposal:

'I would be glad to accept you as a pupil, but first of all I need you to act in a certain manner, so that things may proceed in accordance with their best potentiality. First, I would like you to employ me in a reasonably honourable capacity, within my capabilities and so long as I discharge whatever responsibilities you give me adequately. But you should also, from time to time, in public, reproach or threaten me in such a way as to make it appear that I have no sinecure.'

The governor agreed to do this, remarking only that he was surprised that anyone would wish to be subjected to such a show of insecurity.

The years passed, and in due time, the Sufi gained many disciples and established his own business interests which supported him adequately. In the meantime he had, of course, become well known, and the scholar had expressed the arguments against his teachings, while the lawyer also played his part in putting the other side of the case.

Finally, on the day that he was able to leave the service of the governor, the Sufi called the three other men to his house and, setting a meal before them, informed them all that he was now ready to accept them all as disciples.

'While it is of course the prerogative of the master to teach in whatever way he finds the best,' said the scholar, 'I would like to know why you asked one of us to support you, another to oppose you and the third to threaten you.'

The Sufi said:

'I am perfectly ready to enlighten you as to the reason for your various tasks. First bear in mind that the outward must be firm before the inward can be made firm; and that those of you who were first in accepting me are last in being accepted into the Teaching only because you will need the least actual time in your studies.

'I asked you, the scholar, to put the case against me so that, when the inevitable opposition arose, people instead of mounting an ill-considered campaign against the Way, would leave it to whoever was already adequately representing this point of view. Who better than the logician best able to express all aspects of a case?

'But, since there are always people who are influenced by inimical propaganda, it was necessary that the other side of the matter should be advocated. For this role I chose a respected lawyer who has also a wide culture, to whom people would listen as much as they would to the scholar.

'Like a sponge absorbing surplus water, your mutual action was able to take up the excess controversy which, as always, is rooted in the desire of people to discuss. The argument was therefore safely contained in this manner, and the desires for discussion, which exists as a force in itself, were given appropriate expression. Since neither of you stood to gain repute by his victory, the debate was in the hands of people who would not twist it to personal ends.

'The desire to have a suitable post in the administration of this city was both because of the tradition of our Way that those who pursue it should be gainfully employed and also so that I could contribute towards the good of the people while being a person of adequate status in their eyes, something which a knowledge of their mentality makes necessary. The need to be threatened was based on the fact that in all administrative systems there are people who seek to bribe, suborn or undermine public officials. If my position were thought to be insecure, these people would tend to leave me alone, counting on the likelihood that I would in any case be dismissed before long. Such people's plotting, too, would come to the ears of the governor, my employer, when they tried to influence him further against me, thus exposing their inner characteristics to him, enabling him to take any necessary action. In addition, any plotting which they did amongst themselves seeking my downfall and their promotion would divert their energies and not secretly afflict the State.

'We live in a world where people are quite unaware of the sources of their actions, and the human community is therefore influenced by unreasoning factors. To enlist them in a pattern of defence which shall help those who are trying to achieve good is at least as useful as searching them out and cutting them down, only to allow further weeds of a similar sort to grow up and to have to attack them again. Choosing the latter path, we would never make progress, but only at best remain where we were, clearing weeds and waiting for more to be cleared. Under such circumstances, how could a people make any progress towards the true destiny of man?'

When Bad is Good:
The Legend of Asili

THERE WAS ONCE a man, a simple workman named Asili, who had been prevailed upon to lend some money, all his savings of a hundred pieces of silver, to a wicked trader who promised to invest it and make him a profit on some commercial transaction.

When, however, Asili went to the merchant to see what news there was of his investment, he said: 'Asili? Never heard of you. Money? I have had none of it. Begone, unless you want me to call the police and charge you with demanding money by means of threats...'

Since this workman was unversed in the ways of the world, and had not asked for a receipt or taken care to have witnesses to the matter, he went back to his hut, realising that there was nothing which he could do.

That evening he decided to pray. Going out on the roof of his hovel, he raised his hands towards the sky and said: 'O God, I pray for justice, so that

I may receive back my money which I need at this time; whatever the means which can be employed, for I have no ordinary path open to me.'

As it happened, a certain villainous-looking dervish who was passing heard this prayer. As soon as Asili had finished, the dervish approached him and said: 'I will help you; for everything needs a vehicle, and perhaps your chance of an answer to your supplication comes through me!'

Asili at first shrank from the man, as one who had the reputation of being afflicted with the Evil Eye; and Asili had enough troubles already.

'You may be interested to know, though you may not believe it,' continued the dervish, 'that although people hate me, I do good; just as many of those whom people love do evil. I will take up your case.'

So saying, the dervish went on his way. Not long afterwards Asili was standing near the trader's shop, wondering if there was anything he could do about his money, when the dervish strode into view, and cried out: 'Ah, friend Asili – my old friend! Come to my house this very evening, for I have at last decided to explain some of my secrets to you, and you will know valuable things that I know, and your life will not be the same after that.'

Asili did not even know where the dervish's house was, much less that he was to be selected to receive important secrets. He still felt nervous about the dervish's reputation as an evil man.

The trader, however, who had been attracted from his shop by the noise, was also terrified of the dervish's 'evil eye', and the knowledge that Asili was the disciple of this man threw him into panic.

That evening, while he was sitting at home, Asili found the dervish at his door. 'Well,' he said, 'how much did the trader give you?'

'He gave me five times what he had taken and denied that he had,' said Asili, still rather mystified.

'Well,' said the dervish, 'remember that there are many things which are supposed to work through the power of good but which are in fact based on bad things. There are, similarly, many things thought to work by the power of badness, but in reality these are sometimes good things. A bad man like your trader would not have listened to the admonition of a good man; but bring into play the supposed threat of someone even worse than him, and he is powerless against it. Truly the sages have said: "Good cannot come out of bad. But you have to be sure that it really is bad before you make your clever judgements."'

Too Good to Miss

THERE ARE GROUPS of performers who call themselves dervishes who specialise in eating poisonous snakes, stabbing themselves with sharp knives, and swallowing red-hot coals. They claim that these activities, which have been observed and even filmed by researchers, prove that they are at least partly in another dimension: hence their physical body cannot be harmed by them.

One day, so the story goes, a man who wanted to enter the same ethereal realms came upon a band of these performers, who were swallowing live coals with every evidence of enjoyment, and breathing out smoke and steam.

Carefully copying exactly what they did, the newcomer picked up a handful of coals and gulped them down, without any harm and without feeling anything.

One of the dervishes caught him by the arm. 'Why did you do that?'

'To participate in the sublime ritual...'

'Yes, but why didn't you breathe out the smoke? That's the very best part...'

What Not to Do

THE LEARNING FUNCTION, among the Sufis, is sharply distinguished from the entertainment or emotional stimulus function; something which is seldom understood by outside observers, or, for that matter, by people who want to be stimulated and not to experience any developmental activity. This story seeks to illustrate the point:

A would-be dervish saw a woman grooming a beautiful and well-kept donkey by a roadside and stopped to admire it.

'What are you doing?' he asked her.

'Taking my donkey into town: I always take him with me to market.'

'What is he like to ride?' asked the traveller.

'Oh, I never ride him,' said the woman.

'In that case, why not let me buy the animal?'

She sold it to him and he led it away.

The following week the woman saw him sitting in a corner of the marketplace. 'How is the donkey getting on?' she asked.

'The donkey? It kicks, it throws me off its back, it refuses anything but the finest food – it's hopeless!'

'Ah,' said the woman, 'you must have been trying to ride on him!'

Young and Old

TWO INCIDENTS, SEPARATED by a decade, both of them witnessed by me, as it happened, help to show how one often sees only one part of a process.

I was in the presence of Kaka Anwar, carrying out a period of Service (*Khidmat*), following his instructions in every way.

A highly recommended aspirant to studentship, a man of forty years or so, was announced.

When he had been with us for an hour or two, and the Kaka had not given him the kind of answers he quite evidently desired, he said:

'I am a man of much experience in occult, spiritual and similar matters, and I have visited many reputed sages. You and I do not speak the same language. I must be frank, for "sincerity is the lifeblood of reality": and I say to you that you are still far too young. You are no use to me.'

He went on his way, and Kaka made no comment on the event. Ten years later, having followed his nose, read more books, pursued rumours of sages and attended many a circus, the same man was back at Kaka Anwar's house. As it happened, I was also in the presence of the Master.

Kaka Anwar said to him:

'Is there anything which you want?'

He said:

'It has cost me a decade of my life, but I now realise that it is *you* whom I should have been following.'

'I do not deny it,' said the Kaka, 'but unfortunately there is no place for you. Ten years have passed, during which I *could* have been of use to you. You thought I was too young. Now I find that you are too old. You should have been following me: but now you cannot – for I am no use to you. What you thought was true then, is true now. What you think true now, was true then.'

Never Complain

SOMEONE WAS SPEAKING against Mojudi in a company of those who wished to encounter the Truth.

One of them said: 'Perhaps you have not met or spoken with Mojudi.'

The complainer said: 'I know more about him than you imagine. Not only have I met him and spoken with him, but he has tried to give me shallow and restrictive instructions, none of which will I obey. On the contrary, I want to expose his lack of depth.'

The company was impressed, and they allowed themselves to learn from this man what became, for them, a general opinion about Mojudi.

One day a travelling dervish was at one of their meetings. Hearing the discussion about Mojudi, he asked what the sheikh had tried to get the disaffected student to do.

'He told me that he was prepared to give me a study task on two conditions. The first was that I would never complain or try to wriggle out of it. The second was that I would never, without his permission, leave his teaching or choose any other path to Truth, or try to teach others.'

'And you rejected him on those grounds?'

'And I rejected him on those grounds.'

'But do you not see,' asked the dervish, 'that Nuri Mojudi was not only proposing to provide you with the means to progress, but was also describing all your major characteristics, weaknesses of discontent, complaint, abandonment of something without giving it a chance, trying to choose, without insight, some other path?'

'Then why did I not understand and stay with him? If he knew what I was like, why did he try, unsuccessfully, to get me to join him, when he should, surely, have been able to predict the outcome, this very conversation even?'

'Because there was always the possibility that you would see the situation as he outlined it. And, until you did this, you would be doing good by illustrating by your complaints and arguments, by your denigration of him, how well he had assessed you. You are a living proof of his insight, for those who can see it. For those who do not, like your companions here, you are a walking book that someone like me can come along and read out to them.'

His Lips are Sealed

IT IS SAID that once anyone arrives at the knowledge of the Highest Truth, his lips are sealed against repeating it. All he can do is to try to provoke, without saying why, the experiences in others which he has himself had, so that the teaching may continue by this means. Often he must do this anonymously, or at least without letting others know that he knows what is to befall them. This is encapsulated in this allegory:

There was once a learned physician who only had to close his eyes for the remedy for the illness of any patient to be shown to him in a picture. One day a man came to him and described his symptoms, and the doctor closed his eyes. He saw a picture of the patient eating something noxious, and he realised that he could not possibly prescribe such a medicament, so he merely said: 'I am sorry to have to say to you that you are incurable – go on your way.'

Not long afterwards this sufferer lay down to rest by a roadside, and fell asleep. His mouth fell open, and a poisonous beetle crawled into it. The man woke with a start and tried to spit out the insect, but it stung him before he could eject it. For a time he felt terribly ill, but after some hours he realised that he was cured.

And, in spite of the wise man having tried to protect himself by not speaking of poison, he still became the subject of some ridicule when the story was told. The former sufferer lost no opportunity of telling everyone that he had been cured by a stinging beetle, when the most famous doctor of the day had been unable to do anything for him...

Third Year Studies

ONE OF THE prominent Sufis of Central Asia was examining candidates who wanted to become disciples.

'Anyone,' he said, 'who wants entertainment, not learning, who wishes to argue, not study, who is impatient, who wants to take rather than to give – should raise his hand.'

Nobody moved. 'Very good,' said the teacher, 'now you will come and see some of my pupils, who have been with me for three years.'

He led them into a meditation hall, where a row of people were sitting. Addressing them, he said: 'Let those who wish to be entertained, not to learn, who are impatient and want to argue, the takers and not givers – let them stand up.'

The whole row of disciples got to their feet.

The sage addressed the first group. 'In your own eyes, you are better people now than you would be in three years' time if you stayed here. Your present vanity helps you even to feel worthy. So reflect well, as you return to your homes, before coming here again at some future time if you wish, whether you want to feel better than you are or worse than the world thinks you to be.'

The Man in the White Hat

NIM HAKIM WAS a man of no special distinction. One day he was walking past a house when some people came out and stopped him. 'Please come in,' they said, 'and look upon our mistress, who is sick.'

'Why me?' asked Nim Hakim.

'Because a wise man, long ago, predicted her illness and said: "When she is ill, she will only be cured by the colour white, five feet above the ground." While we were looking for such an object, we saw you with a white hat, realised that you were about five feet tall, and we really want the use of your hat.'

'Strange,' thought Nim Hakim, but he entered the house and stood at the foot of the lady's bed.

A little after looking at him, sure enough, she sat up and was better.

'I am a natural doctor,' said Nim Hakim to himself. He had forgotten that he was only an instrument.

This set in train a strange series of events.

He decided that his present life as a student was a waste of his time. He would go out into the world and make his mark. Nim Hakim went first of all to the baker, and asked him to bake him a loaf of bread for his travels.

And he set off down the road.

Presently he came to a country where nobody had heard of him, and soon learned that the people had a problem.

A certain elephant used to raid the countryside regularly, and trample people to death.

'I have a cure for all ills,' said Nim Hakim to them, and he settled down to wait for the elephant. Presently it came thundering through the streets of the capital.

Everyone ran away. So, too, did Nim Hakim, because he realised that this was rather different from standing at the foot of a sick person's bed. But the elephant caught up with him, bowled him over and started to eat his bread.

As Nim Hakim lay on the ground, stunned, the elephant started to topple over, and the people started to come out of their houses to see what was happening to their champion.

They were just in time to see the elephant keel over and die. Then they carried Nim Hakim in triumph to their King.

What they did not know was that the baker, who hated the superior airs of Nim Hakim, who also owed him a great deal of money, had put in the bread enough poison to kill an elephant.

The King, overjoyed at the deliverance of his people, renamed Nim Hakim, calling him Nim Mulla. Hakim means 'doctor', but Mulla means 'Master': for surely what Nim had done was a feat of mastership rather than of doctoring.

'You may call me Master if you like,' said Nim disdainfully, 'but I demand to be rewarded with the command of all your armies. After all, they have regularly been put to flight in the past by that very same elephant.'

Partly in fear, partly in admiration, and partly through greed to enlist such a formidable man in his service, the King made him 'Marshal of the Armies, Nim Mulla'. And this was his full title.

Time passed, and Nim spent years in preaching his own importance, and having it passed around by those who knew of his exploit.

Quite a lot of people tried to emulate him, but whenever they looked at sick people or tried to kill runaway elephants, they had no success. 'Keep trying,' said Nim. But his followers' failures, as much as his own success, only went to prove that he was in some way a superior man. This, at any rate, was the way it looked to all concerned. Nobody having any other opinion about the matter, Nim was firmly established in his role.

Then one day the country was invaded by a man-eating tiger. Regularly the tiger crept into villages and carried off victims, until the people called upon their hero, the Great Marshal Nim, to deliver them.

At the head of the greatest army the country had ever seen, Marshal Nim marched against the tiger. Finally the maneater was espied by scouts. The troops – as usual – fled in all directions, leaving their leader alone to face the menace. After all, they said to each other, he was a sort of superman, and it was his job to do things like that, not theirs.

Nim, when he saw the tiger with his own eyes, was terrified, and climbed the nearest tree. The tiger settled down to wait for him at the foot of it. The siege went on for days. Every night the tiger roared and Nim trembled, and both got hungrier and hungrier.

After a week, the tiger roared louder than ever, and Nim, weakened by fatigue and hunger, trembled worse than ever. This movement dislodged Nim's dagger from his belt. It fell, just as the tiger was opening his mouth to roar again.

The dagger went straight down the tiger's throat, killing him instantly.

After some time Nim realised what had happened.

'I am clearly the special instrument of Fate, and as such the greatest man alive,' he said to himself. Climbing down from the branches, he returned to the King with the tiger's ears, and was immediately proclaimed the Greatest Champion of the Realm.

Not long afterwards the Greatest Champion received news that the army of a neighbouring country was invading his adopted land. In spite of the miracles which had protected him in the past, this time Nim was frightened. Packing all the gold and silver plate he could find that very night, he mounted a fast horse and rode away, trying to put as many miles as possible between himself and the enemy before dawn.

His horse stumbled in the dark when they were still quite near the enemy's camp. The precious plates fell with a clang upon some rocks. The enemy soldiers, thinking that they had been attacked, rushed to arms and started to fight, hand-to-hand, with one another. So fierce was the battle that they were all killed.

Nim was cowering behind some rocks, too paralysed to move, when scouts from the King's army found him, and carried him back in triumph to the throne-room.

There were no fresh crises during the remainder of his life and he lived to a ripe old age. This is why you hear so much of the Great Nim, who wrought miracles and was never defeated. Every nation, did they but know it, has its Nim, under one name or another, in the distant and romantic past.

Subjective

BECAUSE OF IMAGINATION and the lack of experience in understanding what inner developments signify, people experimenting with different states of consciousness more often than not give garbled accounts of their inward life.

One day a number of disciples were sitting around talking about their experiences. One of them said:

'As I was doing my exercises, I felt as if I had been illuminated by a shaft of light which split my brain into two equal and glowing halves...'

He was interrupted by another who said: 'That reminds me of the time when my brain was split into 90,000 pieces and the greatest mystics in the world came to find out how I had done it.'

There was a shocked silence. Then one of the other pupils said: 'Perhaps you might care to show your humility by asking forgiveness of our friend for such levity.'

'Well,' said the other, 'if our friend cares to do something about the glow of his brain, I shall try to reduce the number of spiritual masters who paid homage to me.'

Final

A VERY UNSUITABLE would-be disciple made his way, with the greatest possible effort, up the winding track to the cave of a hermit who was reputed to have great mystical powers.

When he got there he said: 'I wish only to serve you, and to gain the high illumination which you enjoy, and which you must surely desire to share with the humble people of the world.'

The hermit simply shouted: 'Get out of my sight, this instant!'

So the traveller stumbled down the mountain track, and had just reached the bottom, when he saw the hermit waving and beckoning from his eyrie.

'So,' said the man to himself, 'it was one of those famous tests, applied to assess one's fortitude.' Although he was almost exhausted, he climbed up all the way to where the hermit sat and, panting, threw himself on the ground in front of him.

'And another thing,' said the hermit, 'don't you ever try to come back, with your nonsense about "tests".'

Trial Postponed

THERE WAS ONCE a Sufi, it is said, who was to be tried by jury for undermining the beliefs of the people by writing and saying unsettling things which, it was held by the jurists, should be reserved for higher minds.

Since he was a man of great importance, it was agreed that he could name the kind of people, though not the individuals, who should compose the jury for his case.

He stipulated that they should be:

A scholar, without his teacher's gown, who would admit that his own writings were not authoritative; a dervish whose pride took the form of refusing to accept money on the grounds that it was corrupting, instead of being able to detach from its corrupting effect; a butcher who had not eaten meat for three months; a king who could rule wisely without advisers; and an official who did not want to be addressed with respect.

That was, as they tell it, a hundred years ago, and the jury has not yet been assembled.

The Spring of Life

A MAN ONCE decided to dedicate himself to the search for the Spring of Eternal Life.

'I shall drink from it,' he said, 'and afterwards share the discovery with all mankind.'

After many years he found the Spring. He drank, and he drank, and he drank.

First youth returned to him, and as he drank yet more he became younger and younger, until he became a squealing baby lying by the Spring, crying for more and more to drink.

A woman passing nearby saw the child, and brought him up as her own.

And that is why he was not able to tell anyone where the Spring of Life is.

Not So Many

THE WORLD OF supposedly spiritual people is full of unconsciously hypocritical people.

A self-centred aspirant to higher consciousness was visiting a Sufi centre and paused to speak to the keeper of the gate.

'I was reflecting,' he said, 'how few of us know how many true seekers of the Truth there are in this world...'

'I have been looking after this gate for half a century, and I can tell you something about it,' said the other man.

'Really? Then how many *are* there?'

'One fewer than *you* think there are.'

The Reason...

PEOPLE BECOME VERY impressed by the dietary and other observances of reputed spiritual teachers, and for some reason they also sometimes equate age with sanctity. There is also a tendency to imagine that there can only be one way to higher knowledge, and that anything which conflicts with this must therefore be its opposite, instead of, as is often true, being a suitable alternative. These facts have been woven into an appropriately illustrative tale:

A man who imagined himself to be a genuine Seeker-after-Truth visited a venerable sage who had a great reputation as a spiritual guide, and came from a long line of mystics.

'How wonderful,' he began, 'that you have reached such a venerable age and are so widely and justly admired for your spiritually enhancing austerities. What are the outstanding characteristics of your discipline?'

'First,' quavered the ancient, 'I stick firmly to vegetarianism; and secondly, I am always serene and never on any account lose my temper with anyone or anything...'

He was interrupted by a great noise of shouting and roaring from the direction of the kitchen.

'Take no notice of that,' beamed the implacable one, 'for it is only my illustrious father, beating up the butcher for being late in delivering his meat...'

Another Way of Doing Things

THERE WAS ONCE a king who was a terrible tyrant, and at last a deputation of his people went to a Sufi master, asking him to help them get rid of him.

'Very well,' said the Sufi, 'but I can do nothing direct: I must take advantage of what is there already. Understanding the patterns of life and thought is the work of Sufis.'

Presently he presented himself before the King.

'Great Monarch,' he said, 'I insist that I be killed, three paces in front of your throne, two hours from now.'

The people who were present said to one another: 'What a great man is our Sufi! Undoubtedly he seeks to become a martyr, so that, when the King kills him, the people will rise in fury and dethrone the monster...'

But the King, for whom things were not so obvious, was nevertheless highly suspicious. 'Take the man to the dungeons and put him on the rack until he admits why he really wants to be killed,' he commanded.

Half an hour later the Chief Torturer appeared with his captive before the King and reported: 'He says that it has been foretold that whoever dies on that spot at the time indicated will become the supreme human being of the age.'

The King himself stepped forward: 'Slay me here, immediately!' he commanded – and nobody, of course, dared to disobey his order.

Celestial Fruit

ONCE UPON A time there was a man who was completely obsessed with the search for Truth. He was so determined to find it that he alternately spent his time in praying to be granted Truth and following any clue which he might hear of about it.

But so anxious was this man to find Truth that he did not bother himself to try to improve his own ways of thinking; and he would never stay long enough with one teacher to learn all that he could teach him; always someone else seemed to beckon.

One day this man was walking through the streets of Istanbul when he saw a man in luminescent green walk into a mosque. He remembered that it was said that such a man might be Khidr, and that one should seize his garment and ask him to grant a favour.

He went into the mosque, found Khidr near a pillar, held on to his sleeve, and said: 'Great Khidr, Man of Beyond, grant me the vision of Truth!'

Khidr looked at him and said gently, 'You are not ready for Truth yet.'

But the man insisted, and Khidr said: 'Since you have seized my sleeve, and because some may one day benefit from your story, I shall let you experience Truth. But your fate will be upon your own head.'

Khidr conducted the seeker to a certain house. There in a special room they spent some time in contemplation. Then Khidr took the eager disciple to meet a mysterious robed figure, dressed like a king, and together they travelled in a mysterious boat for illimitable distances, visiting places which one could never describe, and seeing things which man has in the past only dreamed about, but which really do exist in the Reality of Realities.

One day the man said to the King: 'I feel that I would like to return to visit my kindred, and see how man has behaved since I have been away.'

The King said: 'Holy Khidr, my representative, has already told you that you were not ready for Truth. Now you have arrived at the condition in which you may find that you have not understood that there is the eternal and the temporary. If you return now, you will find that there is seemingly nothing left of what you knew.'

'What talk is this?' asked the man. 'For was it not only a few months ago that I left my own village? May I not see my own family again? How can things change in such a space of time?'

The King said: 'You will find out; but you will never now be able to return to us; and Truth, although you have found it, is of no use to you. Perhaps if others can hear of these facts through you, however, it may help you in some way at some time.'

With these cryptic remarks, he gave the disciple a celestial fruit, saying: 'Eat this when you have no other course open to you.' And he instructed one of his lieutenants to return the traveller to his home.

When he arrived there, he found that endless ages had passed. His house was a ruin, and there was hardly anyone who could understand his language. People crowded around him, and he told them his story. They thought that he was either a deranged saint or someone who had descended from heaven.

He could make nothing of the mystery as to why he had not himself aged during what turned out to be many thousands of years' absence. And so, in his perplexity and dissatisfaction, he ate the celestial fruit. No sooner was it in his stomach than he started to become old, and, before the eyes of the people who had found him, he died of old age.

Now there are only a few people who remember this story, and they all imagine that it is nothing more than a legend.

A Gnat's Weight...

A SUFI ONCE annoyed the scholars of a certain country so much that they vied with one another in trying to discredit him. One scholar spoke slightingly of his ancestry; another of the quality of his writings; a third of the frequency of his utterances; a fourth of his silences; a fifth of his associates. In short, you will see that they treated him in the manner traditional in such circles.

In spite of this campaign, students continued to listen to the Sufi. Their questions caused their teachers continued concern. So the scholars changed their tactics.

Some of them went to the King of their country. They said:

'Sire, such-and-such a Sufi is corrupting the minds of your Majesty's subjects. We urge you to do something about him before your own position is threatened.'

The King was perplexed. 'Surely,' he said, 'you wise men can encompass his downfall, for you are, as I have frequently seen, adept at such activities.'

'We have tried, Majesty,' they said, 'but he seems to care nothing for his name, and the consequence is that people are denying the real value of repute itself.'

'Do you suggest that I kill this man and make him a martyr?' asked the King.

'No, indeed that would be the last thing that we should do,' said the scholars.

'Since scholars are the advisers of kings in this country,' said the King (who was aware that he should keep on the right side of these venerable beasts for his own safety), 'advise me, and I will at once put any suitable stratagem into action.'

'What must be done is to demonstrate the fool-ishness of the man, so that people will not want to copy him,' said the most cunning of the scholars.

'How can I do that?' said the King.

'Challenge him with an impossible task,' said the scholar. He provided a suggestion to verify the Sufi claim 'to transcend ordinary limitations'.

And so it was that the Sufi, passing the palace one day, heard a herald announce:

'His Majesty has been pleased to declare that he is prepared to adopt the ways of the Sufi, providing that any Sufi can endure physical hardships that no scholar would accept.'

The Sufi presented himself to the King, who said:

'Sufi, a gnat's weight of demonstration is worth an elephant-load of reputation. Will you take my test?'

'I will,' said the Sufi.

'It is midwinter,' said the King, 'and the nights in the open are unbearably freezing. I propose to leave you, without any clothes or covering, on the roof of the citadel for a whole night. If you are alive in the morning, and not even frostbitten, I will accept that you have abilities which scholars lack.'

The Sufi accepted the challenge without hesitation.

In the morning an immense crowd had collected to see whether the Sufi had survived. As dawn broke they saw that he was not only alive but covered with sweat, rolling a huge boulder, which he had dislodged from the battlements, from one end of the flat roof to another.

As the Sufi was brought down by the guards, the people cheered him to the echo.

'I have created a hero, and you have made me look a fool, you marvellous scholars,' screamed the King to his advisers. 'If I had left him alone there would have been at least a possibility that his ways would not have undermined my throne. Now it looks as if I will have to carry out a sustained campaign to show the people that I am after all intelligent or worthwhile, or something.' And he sat there listening to the cheers of the crowd, biting his nails.

The Sufi appeared and said:

'Your Majesty, come with me to the battlements.'

The King dolefully followed the Sufi to where the populace could see and hear them.

The Sufi said:

'Good people, look upon your wonderful and intelligent King. In order to illustrate to the whole world that scholars who were intriguing for position are limited to literalism, he put me to a test which was really a test of them. I was asked to survive a winter's night on the citadel to prove my Sufihood. But, since scholars are capable only of mental gymnastics, the only answer all would understand was by means of gymnastics.'

When they were alone again, the King said to the Sufi:

'Why should you protect me, when I was trying to disgrace you?'

'Because *you*, your Majesty,' said the Sufi, 'were not really trying to do anything at all, including disgracing me. You were being manipulated by your advisers. If I had caused you to be disgraced, you would not have been a king any more. Now, a king who has learnt a lesson is surely more useful than a beggar who was once a king.'

'But you told a lie when you said that I was trying to expose the scholars,' said the King.

'I was telling the truth, but I was telling it ahead of the time when it was to take place,' said the Sufi; 'because from now on, there can be no doubt, your Majesty will indeed try to preserve our society against such people; and one method which you will undoubtedly employ is that of: "A gnat's weight of demonstration is worth an elephant-load of reputation".'

Grapes

DO YOU KNOW the story of Mulla Nasrudin and the grapes?

Someone once told him:

'Never eat food which is sent you as a gift if you don't know the giver.'

'But then it would be wasted,' said Nasrudin.

'Not at all, Mulla – you try it on the cat first.'

'Then what?'

'If the cat dies, or even refuses to eat it, you know the food was poisoned.'

The Mulla was very much impressed by the logic and great practicality of this new knowledge.

One day he found a basket of grapes left by someone on his doorstep. He called his friend Wali to watch the experiment.

The cat sniffed the grapes, and then walked away.

'We can eat them,' said the Mulla.

'But the cat wouldn't,' said Wali.

'I know, you fool, but what cat *would* eat grapes?'

The Book of the Secrets of the Ancients

SIKANDAR OF BALKH was the owner of huge tracts of land and master of a hundred castles. He had herds of *karakul* sheep and forests of walnuts, as well as the possession of a book of the secrets of the ancients, which had been given him by his father. 'My child,' said his father, 'this is the most precious thing which you have. It will enable you to do things which in these times no ordinary man can do.'

Sikandar Khan had remarried in his middle years a beautiful, inquisitive and self-willed woman named Gulbadan ('Rose-bodied') Begum.

As the years passed, Sikandar started to age. He thought to himself: 'If I could find some formula from the book of the secrets of the ancients which would enable me to become young again, this would undoubtedly be a suitable usage and a great advantage to me.'

He read carefully through the book, and found that there were many things in it, including a means of rejuvenating oneself. The writing was so difficult, and the symbols and words used were so old, that he had to go on frequent journeys to what few ancient sages remained, in order to complete his understanding of the whole process.

Sikandar erected a small pavilion in one of his gardens for the working of the magical process, and spent many days there in repeating formulae, in all manner of exercises prescribed by the book, and mixing the ingredients for the magical drink which was to give him new youth.

All this time his wife Gulbadan was becoming more and more curious about what he was doing. According to the ancient science's laws, however, Sikandar could not tell her the purpose of his actions, on pain of failure. He kept the pavilion securely locked, and allowed nobody to go near it.

Sikandar followed the instruction of the book to the letter. He imported all sorts of rare and interesting playthings and luxuries for Gulbadan, so that her curiosity might be diverted and in the hope that she would become less anxious about his activities.

In order to maintain his own tranquillity, as the book suggested, he engaged himself upon his business and tribal affairs most thoroughly, in addition to attending to the needs of the ancient wisdom.

When the time came that he had completed the processes all but one, Sikandar followed the book's command to go on a pilgrimage to a very distant place in order to hear what was to be said to him by whatever adept happened to be in residence there.

Sikandar made Gulbadan promise not to approach, nor let anyone enter, the pavilion of secrets.

When he arrived at the shrine, he said to the sage who was presiding over it:

'Master, I am so-and-so, and my affair is such-and-such, and my problem is that I cannot carry out the last part of the process, for the book of the ancient wisdom tells me to do something which is against the behaviour of dervishes and which is not consistent with chivalry, and which is forbidden by the Holy Law.'

The sage said:

'My child. The wisdom of the ancients is in arranging and not in commanding. The passage in your book does not recommend you to do anything. It tells you to come on this pilgrimage, and it tells you that a certain ingredient will be needed. It does not say that you have to obtain the ingredient, any more than it tells you to pray at this shrine. The prayer is your invention, and the procuring is your own assumption.

'Each process must go step by step. I advise you to return to your home, now that you have fulfilled the recommendation of the book.'

These words confused Sikandar. If an ingredient was needed, who was to obtain it other than himself? If he was to visit a shrine, what was he to do other than pray there?

But he still retained his determination and his respect, so he kissed the hand of the sage and made his difficult way homewards.

Meanwhile, Gulbadan had told her maid about the locked pavilion. She had not said what she thought it was for, but thought: 'I must tell someone something about this, otherwise I shall burst.'

The maid told a servant whom she met in the bazaar, and this woman told her son, who was a locksmith:

'Some Sikandar Khan, who is on a pilgrimage, has a vast treasure or something else of priceless worth locked in a garden pavilion.'

The locksmith, whose name was Qulfsaz, thought:

'I shall go and see what I can find out about this matter. With my skills I can open and afterwards shut the door so that nobody will know what I have done. Therefore there will be no damage. This does not mean theft, it means information.'

So he went to the pavilion at the dead of night.

As soon as he touched the lock of the door, however, something seized him, and he fell to the ground, writhing and howling in agony.

When the lady of the house walked into the garden the following morning, she found the dead body of the locksmith stretched before the pavilion's door.

The matter was reported to the superintendent of police, who decided that the man had died naturally during an attempted burglary.

Now, a few days later, Sikandar Khan arrived home. He went straight to the pavilion before entering the house, took the substances which were the results of his efforts and set fire to them.

He said to himself:

'The wisdom of the ancients is indeed profound! It teaches how man may attain certain desired ends. But it also shows how impossible it is for him to reach them, because he is not able to do the things which are stipulated.'

Then he went to see his wife, and after he had given her the presents which he had brought, and seen his children, and ordered bonfires, sword-dancing and feasting in thanksgiving for his safe return, he sat alone and at ease with her. Sikandar Khan told his wife:

'Since I have abandoned my foolish project in the pavilion, I may now assuage the pain of your curiosity. I was trying to produce, from the book of wisdom of the ancients, something to become young again. The final ingredient was something which I could not bring myself to add. I carried out the process as far as I could, in the hope that this ingredient had some alternative, inner, meaning. I hoped that during my pilgrimage to the Great Shrine the sage there would help me. But he only said, "you do not have to procure the ingredient."

'So I have returned here and destroyed the whole working of the process.'

Gulbadan said:

'You say that you want to relieve my curiosity, yet you have now produced a greater mystery than before! Whatever can this impossible ingredient be?'

'The ingredient,' said Sikandar Khan, 'is that during the last stages of the experiment – a locksmith should be sacrificed.'

The Nuristanis' Boots

TWELVE NURISTANIS CAME down from the high mountain passes to sell their butter in Kabul. When they got their money, they saw a shop selling pairs of leather boots, of a beautiful kind which they had never seen before.

Each Nuristani bought a pair. When they had got them on, they realised that nobody could see his own boots properly, because he was wearing them. Wanting to taste the joys of looking at the new boots, they sat down in a circle, with their legs stretched out, so that everyone could look at all the boots.

After several hours, people began to get curious at the sight of a dozen Nuristanis sitting with their legs looking like the spokes of a wheel. They did not even look happy.

Someone went up to them and said, 'Why don't you ever get up? Is this how things are done in Nuristan?'

'No,' said the Nuristanis, 'this is how things are done in Kabul, when you get new boots.' Then they explained that, admiring the boots and realising that they were all the same, each man had forgotten whose boots were on whose legs; so they couldn't stand up.

'That's easy enough,' said the Kabuli. He brought a stick, and gave each of the peasants a clout with it, causing them to scramble to their feet.

This is the origin of the Nuristani custom of beating anything of uncertain ownership, to see whether it will run to its master.

The Magic Mountain

IN MAIMANA LIVED Abdulwahab, the son of a villager and a man who decided that he should follow the precept of the Wise, where they have said: 'Service is superior to advice – but action is better than anything.'

Abdulwahab heard the villagers saying that they would not long be able to continue paying the heavy taxes demanded by their Khan; that the great dam upon the hill, which supplied water for their valley, would one day collapse, and they badly needed a new mosque.

He also noticed that the local wise man, whose name was Pishki, used to say, every time he heard any of these complaints:

'If only one of you would follow my advice, all these problems would be removed from you.'

Abdulwahab's decision was that he would take the advice, and that he would carry out whatever actions were recommended by the sage.

So he went to Pishki and said:

'May I be your sacrifice! I am a member of this community, and I await your commands if you wish to give any orders which will enable the whole village to be saved.'

Pishki said:

'You have not much time, so be prepared to start at once. This is what you must do:

'You will climb the highest mountain and bring down the feather of the greatest eagle. This you must take to the Humai bird, who will give you a spear. You must cut yourself with the spear and give some of the blood to someone as a charm. Then you must take ordinary bread and model it in the form of a man, and have someone eat it. After that you must journey to a place called The Holy. There you will say things that people do not like. Never mind what they are: whatever the people believe, tell them the opposite.

'When you have done all these things, return to the village, and you will find that your actions have affected matters in such a manner that all is well and the problems which overshadow us have been removed.'

Abdulwahab did everything just as it was detailed to him, although it took three years. He had one adventure after another, and even attracted numerous disciples, since his repute as the 'enigmatic Sage' and the 'man with a sense of purpose' had such an effect upon so many people whom he met.

Then he returned to the village.

He said, to the first villager whom he met:

'I have just come from far away, and have brought down from the highest mountain the feather of the greatest eagle. This I gave to the Humai bird, in exchange for a spear.'

The villager said:

'Madman! We have no time for such as you – we are preparing a celebration – for the villainous Khan is dead!'

'That was my doing!' shouted Abdulwahab.

'Out of my way, liar...' said the villager.

Then Abdulwahab saw the local holy man.

'Mulla,' he said, 'I have to report that we may expect, through my exertions, that the dam on the hillside will not now collapse!'

The Mulla looked at him sadly, and said:

'My son, you have been absent a long time, and it seems as if your wits are absent still. While you were away the streams filling the dam dried up. We found that the old wells near the village were full of water instead. So we do not care whether the dam collapses or not.'

'That was my doing!' shouted Abdulwahab.

'Yes, yes,' said the Mulla, humouring him.

Then Abdulwahab saw the Imam of the local mosque.

'Imam!' he shouted. 'You need not now wait for a new mosque, for you will have one almost at once, since I have arranged it through my exertions!'

The Imam said:

'We do not need a second new mosque.'

Abdulwahab exclaimed:

'You haven't got a first new mosque yet!'

'But we have,' said the Imam; 'for while you were away there was a rich man who came and handed us many bags of gold for a new mosque. It was on the day that I found a piece of bread modelled into the form of a man. I told the rich man and he said: "If there are such idolators around, you should have a new mosque."'

'It was my doing!' said Abdulwahab.

But nobody would believe him.

Abdulwahab went to see the Sage Pishki about the matter, but when he reached the old man's house he found that he was dead.

The Boy Who had a Dream

THERE WAS ONCE a boy named Haidar Ali Jan, whose tutor was a wise old dervish. His father sent him every day to the house of the dervish, who knew almost everything. But all the dervish would teach Haidar was:

'When you have a dream and remember it when you wake up, never tell it until someone says: "May you live forever!"'

When the dervish had been teaching him for some time, Haidar's father said: 'Is the Wise One instructing you in many sciences?'

'No,' said Haidar, 'he is repeating only a single lesson, about dreams.'

'About dreams, indeed!' said his father. He stopped the boy going to any more lessons.

He went to see the dervish and said: 'Why have you wasted my money and my son's time, teaching him only one thing, and that about dreams, of all things?'

The dervish said: 'I teach every student what he needs in his life, preparing him for the most important experience which is to befall him.'

But the father was not satisfied. The explanation made no sense to him. 'You are as bad as the charlatans who pretend that a single exercise, if persevered in, can be applied to all men,' he said, 'only you are slightly more sophisticated.'

Not long after this Haidar had a dream. The next morning he told his mother. She asked him what kind of dream it had been. But since she had not first said: 'May you live forever!' the boy could not tell her. She became quite angry, and sent him to his father.

'What do you want?' asked his father.

'Last night I had a dream,' said Haidar, 'and when I mentioned it to my mother she got angry and sent me to you.'

'What was the dream?' said the father.

Because he did not say: 'May you live forever!' Haidar said: 'I cannot tell you what my dream was.'

So his father became angry with him and said:

'You know the tree at the crossroads where nobody ever passes? You shall go and sit in the branches of that tree as a punishment for refusing to answer a question.'

Haidar set off and climbed the tree. He had not been sitting there long when two travellers stopped in the shade to share a meal.

One said to the other: 'The King has sent for me to answer a conundrum. I cannot understand it, but I dare not refuse to appear at Court. If only the earth would open and receive me, so that I might disappear from the sight of men! If only someone could be sent from Above who could answer this question so that I need not!'

The other traveller said: 'What is this insoluble riddle?'

'The riddle,' said the first traveller, 'is this. There are two pieces of wood and the King, for some purpose of his own, wants to know which of them is made from the root of a tree and which from a bough.'

Haidar jumped down from his branch and said: 'Take me to the King!'

'You may have been sent from Above,' said the astonished traveller, 'so I shall take you with me.'

When they arrived at the gates of the King's capital, Haidar said to his companions, 'Buy a goat, a donkey and a camel.'

At the entrance to the palace the three were stopped.

'We can only let the first traveller in, for he alone has an invitation from the King.'

The first traveller entered and he said to the King, 'I cannot answer your question, Sire, without my companions.' The King said, 'If they can satisfy the *Rais-i-Tashrifat* (Chief of Ceremonials), let them be brought.'

The scholars who had been unable to answer the King's question about the pieces of wood feared that these newcomers might provide the solution. They said to the Rais-i-Tashrifat: 'Here are some questions for the visitors. If they cannot answer, you can exclude them from the Court on the pretext that they lack the necessary finesse.'

The Rais called Haidar and the other traveller, who came forward leading their animals. He said: 'You are not big enough to know how to answer a question.'

Haidar said: 'The camel, who is as of our party, is big enough. A camel was large enough for the Prophet.'

The Rais said: 'You have no beard, how can you know anything?'

Haidar said: 'The goat has a beard, if beards are needed.'

The Rais said: 'You are not a man.'

Haidar said: 'If a man is needed, here is one,' and he pointed to his companion.

The Rais said: 'How can you bear the weight of the responsibility of knowledge, you puny weakling?'

Haidar said: 'Here is another member of our group, a donkey. An ass was fit for the responsibility of carrying Jesus...'

People were laughing and the Rais did not want to appear more foolish, so, muttering 'Let the pedants look to their own worries', he led Haidar through to the audience hall.

When he arrived before the throne, Haidar said: 'Where is the wood?'

Two sticks were brought and Haidar called for a bowl of water.

He threw the wood in. One stick floated. 'That is from the branch,' said Haidar. The other sank. Haidar said: 'And *that* is from the root.'

The King was amazed, for Haidar had divined the roots correctly.

He said to Haidar: 'How did you come upon such an art? It has been prophesied that the man who can tell one stick from another will become my Prime Minister, and save our community from peril.'

Haidar said: 'Glorious Majesty! I had a dream.'

'May you live forever!' said the King. 'And what was the dream?'

'The dream,' said Haidar, 'was that I was called upon to discover which stick was from a root and which from a branch, and that I solved the problem in the manner which you have just seen.'

Belief

A Sufi was once faced with a band of visitors who had travelled an immense distance to sit at his feet. Their belief in his perfection and infallibility had given them the strength to scale mountains, cross deserts, navigate oceans and endure all the hardships which had been their lot.

When they arrived in his presence, they threw themselves on their faces before him, begging to be allowed to devote themselves exclusively to his service.

'Do you believe in me and in whatever I might say?' the Sufi asked them.

They answered:

'We do, everything, and implicitly!'

'Very well,' said the Sufi, 'I shall now test the depth of that belief.'

'Test us, Master!' cried the devotees.

The Sufi continued:

'Now listen to this claim: "I am not here at all." Can you believe that, implicitly?'

The would-be disciples hesitated, and then, one by one, they confessed that they were unable to believe that he was not there.

The Sufi said:

'Although you have been motivated and sustained by feelings, you are really men of words. Your feelings cannot keep pace with your words. You say "I can believe anything", which is words. When you are asked to believe something, you cannot, which shows the lack of deep feelings.

'You are false even to your own assertions.'

Camel's Head

AJIB THE THIEF one day found a camel's head on a rubbish dump. He took it home and wrapped a piece of silk around it, and took it to the market to sell.

The silk merchants looked at the bulky parcel, and one after another offered him such a low price that it was no more than the worth of the actual silk without the bulk represented by the camel's head.

'All right,' said Ajib at length to one of the rascally merchants, 'I'll accept your price, which seems fair enough to me.'

'The man is a fool,' thought the merchant. Aloud he said: 'Is there anything inside the silk to bulk it out?'

Ajib said: 'Camel's head!'

The merchant thought, 'He's getting angry, so I'd better pay him quickly, in case he sells this heavy bundle to someone else.'

So he paid Ajib.

Some days later he saw Ajib in the street and took him at once to the summary court, charging him with false pretences.

'When you were asked whether there was anything inside that bundle, why did you say "No"?' asked the merchant.

'You may have heard me say "No", but what I actually said was "Camel's head!"' said Ajib. 'I imagine that you heard me through your greed, not your ears.'

Case dismissed.

The Horse-Khan, Son of a Khan

ONCE UPON A time there was a great Khan, and this Khan had three beautiful daughters. The first was called 'Silk', the second was called 'Pearl', and the third, the youngest, was called 'Zephyr'.

One day the Khan said to the three girls:

'Come, daughters, it is time that you were married. The first shall marry my court poet, who is also a great swordsman, the second shall marry my standard-bearer, who is also a valiant knight. As to the third one... well, I shall come to that later.'

The two girls were duly married, and the celebration of their weddings occupied twice forty days and forty nights, with sherbets and bonfires, feasts of jollity, gifts and everything that could make a great occasion.

Then the Khan said to some of his men, 'I am tired of all this frivolity. I think that I shall go hunting.' They all set out, accompanied by a splendrous retinue, and arrived at a ruined castle on a hill. 'We shall camp here for the night,' said the Khan.

No sooner had he laid himself down to rest than a huge Dev, a giant ogre, came rising straight out of the ground, and towered in front of him.

'Peace upon you!' muttered the Khan.

'How fortunate that you should have saluted me. If you had not, I would have eaten you alive!' roared the Dev.

'What can I do for you?' asked the Khan.

'There is, alas, nothing that anyone can do for me now,' said the Dev, 'because I have been trapped in a deep well just below where you are sleeping, and I am allowed out only at night, when there is nobody awake to terrorise.'

'I am glad about that,' said the Khan, 'but who is it that has the power to catch and imprison the enemies of man in this amazing manner, since Sulaiman the Son of David (upon whom be Peace) is no more upon the earth?'

'Do you remember the meek dervish who called and saluted you during your daughters' wedding celebrations?' asked the Dev. 'Well, it was him.'

'That dervish?' exclaimed the Khan. 'But he did nothing to me, although I did not obey his instructions in any particular.'

'You have a second chance,' said the Dev, 'because he always tells one twice. He told me to give up my abominable ways twice, too, but I did not believe that he had any powers.'

So saying, the Dev gave a deep sigh. 'I must return to my well now,' he said, and sank back into the ground.

The next morning the Khan woke at dawn and immediately returned to his capital. No sooner had he sat down in his audience chamber and the drums announcing the durbar began to beat, than the same inoffensive-looking dervish presented himself for an audience.

'O Khan!' he said. 'I have come to give you a present. You have married your daughters off in haste. I agree that it was to worthy men, but it was without consulting a dervish.'

'Yes,' said the Khan, 'I am sorry about that.'

'Well,' said the dervish, 'you now have another chance, but it will be a hard one. Take this horse and marry your daughter to it.'

The Khan was not sure whether he could believe his ears, but he decided that he should do as he was commanded.

He sent his daughter to the horse's stable, and made her live there.

What he did not know, and neither did anyone else, was that as soon as Zephyr entered the stable, it was transformed into a beautiful and luxurious bower. And the horse was really a magical man, a youth who could change into human form again only when he was with a beautiful maiden.

'I am myself a Khan and the son of a Khan,' he told her, 'and I am here to teach trustworthiness. This is the only way in which it can be done. Remember, therefore, that no matter how tempted, you must never disclose that I am a man.'

Zephyr promised him, and even when there were rumours that she was married to a horse, or to someone beneath her, she said nothing.

Now the day came when the Khan announced the annual feast and fair at which the most valorous men in the land were to compete in feats of arms. The Ladies Pearl and Silk looked admiringly upon their husbands as they rode into the arena, mounted on wonderful chargers, to defend their titles as the foremost warriors in the land.

'We have heard something about *your* husband, sister,' they said to Zephyr, 'but perhaps this is a time to watch manly daring and admire excellence in combat, rather than to talk of mysterious things.'

In bout after bout, contest after contest, the court poet and the standard-bearer overcame their opponents. The applause was heard from Herat to Badakhshan, and the clanging of spears, the buzzing of arrows and the clash of swords was mingled with the thundering of hooves and the flashing of accoutrements as the champions prevailed again and again against the men of all High Asia.

And, as one bout followed another, as one gasp of excitement, one round of applause, one cry of triumph, followed another, Bibi Zephyr found herself more and more wishing that she could say that her husband was a Khan, son of a Khan, and could – if he wished – beat all comers on the field that day.

The contests were to last three days, and on the second night the horse-Khan said to his wife: 'Khanum, I shall take the field tomorrow. I know how much you have yearned to see me acquit myself. Tomorrow you shall. But let me warn you, this will be a severe test, for both of us. Tell nobody that I am your husband, no matter how strong the temptation. And, if anything should go wrong, take these three horse-hairs. If you need me, burn one of them. Remember, too, that there are only three of them.'

The next morning, as the heralds were announcing the names of the champions left in the contests, a strange knight with a steel skullcap and a crimson turban wound around his face, almost covering it, incomparably well mounted, rode into the arena.

When Zephyr saw that his banner showed only a huge horseshoe, she knew that it must be her husband.

The horse-Khan took on his two brothers-in-law both at once, wrestling on horseback, and with the blunted lance, the long sword and the dagger. He vanquished both of them in a few minutes. Zephyr's sisters were half in tears and half excited to know who the mysterious stranger was.

As he went on to dispose of all the champions, sometimes one by one, sometimes in groups, Zephyr could not restrain herself any longer and she told her father, sitting beside her:

'That is the Khan, the son of a Khan, and he is my husband, married to me in the form of a horse. He is a magical man, here to try our patience.'

The Khan, remembering that the horse had been given to him by the dervish, said:

'This is a serious business, daughter. You have broken your word and failed the test. I fear for you and for us, for it is we who have trained you so badly that faults have become apparent under stress.'

As he said this, the horse-Khan left the field.

That evening, when she went to her apartments, the Bibi Zephyr found a letter from her husband. It said:

'I knew by the weakness which seized me on the field today that you have told someone my secret. I have had to go, and I may never see you again.'

Zephyr was beside herself with grief. Suddenly she remembered the three hairs, and burned one.

Immediately the Dev from the well, which her father had seen on the hunting trip, appeared. 'I did not want you,' said Zephyr.

'You must have been thinking some evil thought as you burned that hair,' said the Dev, 'because that is how these things work.'

'How can I get rid of you?' asked Zephyr.

'Only by calling the dervish,' said the Dev.

Zephyr used her second hair to make the dervish appear. Within a few seconds he had banished the Dev to his well, and had himself vanished.

And then she thought as hard as she could, and burned the third hair, asking for her husband to come. When he appeared, he said:

'Now there is no more that we can do. I am no longer a horse, but an ordinary man, and a Khan, son of a Khan again. We can now live happily until the end of our days. But never forget that if we had been able to use the three magical hairs better and not spend them on our own welfare, it would have been better for everyone.'

Tigers

THERE WAS ONCE a Sufi who was the companion of a certain king. The King said to him:

'I cannot understand your philosophy, just as I cannot help admiring Sufis, as the most interesting people whom I ever meet.'

The Sufi said to the King:

'Tell me one of your difficulties in understanding.'

The King said:

'How, for instance, can a sound affect a person, especially a cultivated person, more than a word? Any animal can make a sound. Words are a higher form of utterance.'

The Sufi said:

'When you are in a suitable condition, I shall demonstrate to you what this may mean.'

Now one day the Sufi and the King were on a tiger-hunt. The King, who was a most talkative person, would not keep quiet, and repeatedly forgot not to raise his voice. Tiger after tiger was frightened away.

The hunter who was with the party at length came to the Sufi while they were resting, bowed low and said:

'When skill and repute fail, it is said that the

only recourse of man is to the Wise. Could your Presence not perhaps prevail upon his Majesty to remain silent when we are stalking tigers? This unworthy individual craves your help, for if we do not bring back a tiger from this hunt, it is I who will get the blame for the King's own shortcoming, and my wife and children, as well as my reputation as a hunter, will suffer.'

The Sufi agreed to help the hunter. When they had caught up with the King again, he saw that the monarch was still talking.

Then the Sufi said, softly, 'Ti...'

At once the King was as silent as a grave, and he whispered so low that even a tiger could not have heard: '...gers?'

The Sufi said:

'Now that Your Majesty has deigned to become silent for a moment, at the sound "Ti...", and even contributed the nonsensical sound "...gers?", allow me to say that words such as "please be quiet", or "if we talk we shall scare the tigers away", or even "hush!" have had no effect all day on someone who claims that words are superior to sounds. Furthermore, please note that people generally know very well what other people mean. "I cannot understand" may be composed of words, but it does not really mean anything once we test it. I have just tested your "I do not understand what you mean by your philosophy".'

Unsolved

Two worthies of the Land of Fools heard that someone called the Polite Man was visiting their capital.

Desiring to meet him, they went to the city's main square. Here they saw a stranger sitting on a bench.

'Do you think that it's him?' one asked the other.

'Why don't you go and ask him?'

The first man went up to the stranger and said:

'Excuse me, but are you the Polite Man?'

The stranger answered:

'If you do not leave me alone, I'll smash your face in!'

The enquirer went back to his companion.

'Well, was he the man we're looking for?'

'I don't know – he didn't tell me!'

Gourou, The Perspicacious Mouse

ONE EVENING A mouse named Gourou was scampering through a house when he heard the sound of children crying. Feeling sorry for them, and also being quite inquisitive, he stopped. He saw a sad sight. The father of the family was trying to light a fire, but the wood was damp.

'Can I help you?' said the mouse.

The man was too worried to be very surprised at being spoken to by a mouse, so he just said: 'If you have straw, you can help me. I must feed these children, but there is no kindling to start the fire.'

So Gourou ran to his nest and brought the man several pieces of dry straw. Soon the fire was blazing and the children were being fed. They were all happy.

'I am a real benefactor,' said Gourou, 'and I deserve something for this.'

'Of course you do,' said the man. He promised to tell his children the story of Gourou the Mouse, the great benefactor, who appeared as if by magic and gave them just what they needed.

'Fame is wonderful,' said Gourou, 'but I want something more tangible as well.'

So the man gave him a large piece of freshly baked bread.

Gourou carried it away. Usually it took him days to collect as much food as this, and all for a few wisps of straw. Wonderful!

He decided to follow up any sign of human beings in distress in future, in case it might prove profitable. Already he saw himself as an individual with a special mission.

The very next morning he was creeping along the floor of the house next door when he heard some children crying. Gourou scampered up to them.

'Children, what is the matter?'

'Our father is a tinsmith,' said one of the little ones, 'and he has gone to his shop to try to earn some money to buy food for us. But we are hungry, and that is why we are crying.'

Gourou had an idea. 'I have some bread,' he said, 'and I will give it to you. What can you give me in exchange?'

When he carried the bread to the children, they were overjoyed, and said: 'Take this tin cup. We are sure that our father would want you to have something in return for such a kind action.'

Gourou took the cup. As he dragged it away, he called back at them, 'Remember Gourou the Perspicacious Mouse, and what he did for you.'

But by then the children were fed and laughing, and all the more so to see a mouse pulling a tin cup.

'Never mind,' said Gourou to himself, 'it is not how it looks to others, but what it looks like to me. I have proved that I am a benefactor. Have I not just given away several days' food in return for a piece of metal?'

He had to take the cup out through the front door of the house, because it was too large to get into his hole from inside. As he was manoeuvring the cup under the large crack in the doorstep, he heard an argument in the dairy across the road. Gourou left his cup and went to see what it was all about.

He found the dairyman trying to milk a cow into his shoe. In this way he lost a lot of the milk as he carried it to the pail.

'What are you doing?' shouted Gourou.

'My milking-pail has rusted away,' said the dairyman, 'and this pail is too high to get under the cow. So I am using my shoe as a milking-pail.'

'You are losing a lot in that manner, friend,' said the mouse. 'Supposing I were to give you a nice, new, shiny cup, would you like that?'

'Very much,' said the milkman.

So Gourou gave the man the cup, and he was able to finish the milking easily.

Soon he had forgotten Gourou, and the mouse ran up to him as he was leaving the dairy. 'What about my share?' he cried.

The man began to laugh. 'You are only a mouse. I have got the milk, and I have put the cup out of your reach. You cannot have anything. It is bad business to do something without first having a contract.'

'But there was a verbal contract,' protested Gourou.

'Then take me to court,' laughed the man, 'who would believe *you*?'

'Just for that,' stormed the mouse, 'I will demand your cow in payment, no, nothing less!'

'Ho, ho!' roared the dairyman. 'All right, then, if you can take the cow away, you can have her.' And he staggered out of the dairy with tears of laughter rolling down his cheeks.

As soon as the man had left, Gourou spoke to the cow.

'Listen, mother: you heard what your owner said. I am your master now. You must follow me, and treat me as you did him.'

'That sounds fair enough,' mooed the cow, 'providing that you give me somewhere to stay and something to eat when I need it. You must also milk me when I need it.'

'We will attend to those details when we come to them,' said Gourou; 'but meanwhile you must follow me.'

And he led the cow out of the dairy, holding on to the end of her rope.

Of course, he could not get the animal into his tiny hole, so he decided to head for the open country, to see what Fate might have in store for him.

Before very long he found that the cow was leading him, because she kept on straying from one patch of juicy grass to another. The mouse had become so important in his own eyes, however, that he said to himself, 'Since I have no real home now, any direction is better than none. This being so, we cannot truly say that the cow is leading me. What counts is who holds the free end of the rope.'

In this way the cow pulled the mouse farther and farther into the countryside.

Some of the people whom they met were amused, some amazed, and Gourou soon became clever enough to cry out whenever a cowherd was seen and to shout: 'That's right, keep on,' or, 'Good, turn left here,' just after the cow had made some move or other.

But the cow was becoming a real burden. For one thing, the mouse could find little food to his taste in the pastures favoured by the cow. Furthermore, there was always the threat of milking time and he had no answer to that.

As he was thinking about this, while still calling out, 'Good, stop here!' and 'Fine, just finish up that tuft of grass!' he saw a small group of soldiers camped in a glade. The cow and the mouse stopped near to them, and Gourou asked them what they were doing.

'If a mouse can understand,' said the leader, 'we are a special group of the King's guards. As we have not been paid for months we are at the point of mutiny. And, to top it all, we have been given the chore of escorting that princess over there, in the sedan chair, to her father's summer capital for the hot weather.'

'No ordinary mouse, if you please!' said Gourou with a courtly bow which quite impressed the soldiers. 'I am Gourou, the Perspicacious, of whom you may have heard under various names, such as The-Mouse-With-The-Cup, The-Giver-of-Bread-Mouse, The-Firemaking-Mouse – and so on.'

'And what can you do for us,' asked the chief of the soldiers, 'for we have a fire, and nothing to drink out of a cup. Furthermore, you do not appear to have enough bread with you to suffice us.'

'My benefactions,' said Gourou, 'are always based upon exchange, for this is the system which has stood me in good stead. It might almost be said that I have discovered the principle that "All things work by exchange".'

'We have nothing to give you,' said the soldiers, all together.

'But you have,' said Gourou; 'give me your burden – the princess. Then you can desert, sell your arms, eat or sell the cow and generally re-arrange your lives.'

'Desertion is a serious crime against our Lord the King,' said the first soldier.

'No mouse ever owned a cow,' said the second soldier.

'It would be nice to be free again,' said the third soldier.

'What has the cow got to say about it?' asked the fourth soldier.

'I want to know more about "All things work by exchange",' said the fifth soldier.

But the leader said, 'This seems like a strange and probably beneficent intervention of Fate in our lives. Men, we shall take the cow, for I refuse to bear this hardship any longer.'

So they took the cow, milked her and had a drink: and they disappear from our story.

The mouse sat politely outside the palanquin for some time, and finally the princess drew the curtain. Seeing that the soldiers were gone, she began to weep, for they were in the middle of a wilderness.

'Your Highness,' said Gourou, 'you are now my bride, by virtue of the principle, discovered by me, and continuously and successfully applied, known as "All things work by exchange".'

'This is absurd,' said the princess. 'Mice do not talk. If they do, they don't know anything about principles. If they do, they cannot exchange things for kings' daughters. Life is better arranged than that!'

But the mouse, by patience and sweet talk, and because there seemed no alternative to his version of the affair, made the princess follow him to a hole under a rotten tree which he had espied during his talk with the soldiers, and considered to be a safe and pleasant bridal home.

'Enter the home of Gourou the Benefactor,' he said to his bride.

'You may be very clever,' said the princess, 'but you have forgotten that a human being cannot enter a mousehole.'

'Then you can stay outside,' said Gourou, rather annoyed. 'Sleep under that brushwood.'

'But I must have food.'

'You can eat those carrots growing in that field.'

'I am a princess, not a gnawing animal. I need sugarplums, and delicate things to eat.'

'"All things work by exchange",' said Gourou, 'and if you need those things, you will have to gather wild fruits and take them to market, sell them and buy what you need.'

The next morning at dawn the princess awoke and started to collect wild fruits. She made a bundle from her veil and she and Gourou started off for the market, which was in the city where her father ruled.

As they entered the city, the princess began to cry:

'Buy my wild fruits, for I have to have sugar-plums; "All things work by exchange" – my bridegroom will give me none.'

The King, hearing his daughter's voice, sent out a party of his guards to bring her to the palace. The mouse concealed himself, and when she appeared in the audience chamber he stepped forward.

'Great King, father-in-law, greeting! I claim my bride.'

'By what right is she your bride?' asked the King, although he had already heard of the tale from the princess.

'By the right of the immutable law: "All things work by exchange". You got this city by an exchange of lives. You protect the people, they give you money in exchange. If a mouse starts to exchange, everyone mocks and says it is impossible. I appeal in the Name of the unchangeable law: flout it if you dare.'

The King turned to his ministers, who counselled him:

'Majesty, although we have never before heard of this law, upon reflection, we cannot see any case which does not fit it. We therefore conclude that it is indeed a hitherto unobserved but nonetheless immutable Law.'

'Is there none who will deliver me from this opinionated mouse?' the King cried in anguish: and all the more so because the doctors of the Law were looking upon Gourou as someone who, having produced a new Law, might present them with another one at any moment.

Then a certain dervish, who had been at the court for many years but had never spoken except in riddles, stepped forward and whispered into the King's ear.

The monarch's brow cleared, and he announced: 'The Doctors of the Law have spoken well, and the Dervish has spoken well! Cause the Mouse Gourou to be proclaimed my son-in-law by virtue of the Great, Immutable Law of "All things work by exchange". This Law is henceforward to be applied throughout my realm. It will first be tested in this our Court.'

Then the King called Gourou to come forward and seat himself beside him. Gourou ran up the steps of the throne and started to perch on the brass platter beside the King. But under this was a brazier, and Gourou was badly scorched. He appealed to the King:

'How can I sit there, O King, for it is too hot for me?'

'It is the custom of this country that the son-in-law must sit beside the King. This is his place.'

He picked up the mouse and held him over the heat.

In a few seconds Gourou felt as if he were roasting, and cried out: 'Who will exchange this terrible heat for the hand of a king's daughter?'

'I will take it back,' said the King, and he let the mouse go. Gourou scampered away as fast as he could, until he had quit the land.

'You gave me advice,' said the King to the dervish, 'and in exchange I bestow upon you the hand of the princess. For, after all, is it not a law that "All things work by exchange"?'

Will it Work?

ONCE UPON A time there was a man who decided that he was wasting his life by having a house, a car and a job. So, instead of having somewhere to live, something to get him around, and something to do, he only had to worry about which hedge he slept under, whether he had corns on his feet, and whether he was doing his ritual mantrams and wearing the right spiritual clothes and eating the latest miracle foods.

Then he came across a really wise man, and to him he said:

'I feel that I have been wasting my life, because since I stopped wasting my life by conventional activities, I have just carried on unconventional but equally stereotyped "spiritual" ones.'

'I can tell you what to do,' said the really wise man. 'You should stop relying on chants, dress and diet; stop imagining that music, incense or dancing, horoscopes, books of divination or perfumes, crazy companions and so on will do you any good, if you want to have knowledge.'

'Marvellous,' gasped the disciple, 'and will this make me truly wise?'

'No,' said the wise man, 'but in comparison to what you were like before, you automaton, it will seem like it.'

Alim the Artful

FROM BADAKHSHAN TO Sarandib, from Marrakesh to Zanzibar, among the Bedouin and the Kochi, wherever the palm tree has been carried, and wherever it will not take root – you will hear of the fame of Alim the Artful.

While there is still a sultan's palace upon this earth, the tales of Alim the Artful will be told and retold. Because to tell a tale of Alim is to bring the shadow of the celestial Humai bird, with honour and good health, upon the teller. And when there is no palace of a sultan, fortune and success will descend upon the hearers as well as the tellers of the tales of Alim, Alim the Artful, blessings upon his memory.

HOW ALIM BOUGHT AN ORCHARD

Now Alim was born in Paghman, the smiling land of the Afghans where the fruit is so delicious that people have been advised not to eat it in case, travelling elsewhere, they might feel the unworthy sentiments of despair and dislike by contrast.

Alim was in Paghman when he heard that there was an orchard for sale. The man who told him this said: 'Alim, you are so cunning that it is said that you can make a demon believe that it is a fairy. You always help people: will you go to the owner of the orchard and use your golden tongue to get it for me at a very low price?' And he pressed a sum of money into Alim's hand to pay for the orchard.

Now this man was a greedy and unworthy individual, whom Alim decided was not fit to have the orchard. He went, nevertheless, to see the owner, and spent some time with him. Presently he came past the house of the greedy man, who said: 'Alim, how did the matter fare?'

Alim said: 'The deal is done.' And the other man jumped for joy. Alim continued: 'I talked and talked and talked. The man at first wanted a high price; then I got it down. Then I got it down again, and again. Then I made him reduce the price by a number of criticisms. Then I suggested that I might want it for the Khan, who as you know is a Sayed, and so he reduced it again. And then I told him that I understood that there might be a new tax on orchards...'

And he went on in this vein for some time, while the greedy man became more and more excited, and – unable to contain himself, shouted, 'How much did you get it for?'

'Less than one-tenth of the price which you were offering, which was itself niggardly enough,' said Alim.

'My dear, dear friend, how can I ever thank you?' asked the greedy man. 'I must reward you with something like one-half of a per cent of the amount.'

'You have already rewarded me enough,' said Alim.

'And how is that?'

'Well, it was the memory of your frugality which kept me going through all that bargaining.'

'If you say so, I shall certainly not press you,' said the greedy man.

'In fact,' said Alim, 'I was so obsessed by your need to save money that I saved *all* your money, in case you had second thoughts.'

'What do you mean, saved all my money?'

'Quite simple. When the price had gone down almost to nothing for that very valuable orchard, I thought "My friend has now saved so much on this deal that it would only be poetic for him to save it all." And so I bought the orchard for myself. Here is your money back.'

HOW ALIM BECAME A THIEF

Alim the Artful travelled to Samarkand, to find that matters were such that all the honest men were in jail and all the thieves had become rich, famous and respected. Because of the corruptness of the Khan, and the example of the Court, the scholars were thieves, the merchants were thieves, the soldiers were thieves and the officials were thieves. Of course, because of their dishonesty, they called themselves the Elect.

Alim said to himself: 'If all the honest men are in jail, then I will become a thief. A thief who knows that he is one must surely be better than one who does not. Furthermore, has it not been said that "In a rose-garden be a rose, in a thicket be a thorn"?

'A thief,' Alim thought, 'should start somewhere. Since I have the option, I shall become Thief to the Grand Khan.'

He went to the palace by dead of night and found the treasury. But there was nothing in it. The Khan knew his own people so well that he had hidden his wealth in a safe place. Search as he might, Alim the Artful could not find anything of value. So he returned to his caravanserai and kept his ears open.

The merchants who regularly used the serai talked among themselves of the collection of emeralds which the Khan was amassing. 'Nobody knows where he keeps them,' said the merchants to one another, 'but he must keep them somewhere. And since nobody can be trusted here, they must be somewhere near him.'

'Quite right,' said Alim to himself. Although he was artful, his maxim was 'Artfulness is not only used, it is learnt'. So a few nights later he was in the palace again, this time by the Grand Khan's bedside.

Alim sat down on a stool near the Khan's head, and started to stroke his forehead. Then he said: 'Can you hear me, Great Khan?' After a few repetitions, the Khan started to answer him. The Khan said: 'What is it?'

Alim said:

'Where do you keep the collection of emeralds?'

'Now, fellow,' said the Khan still in his sleep, 'do you really expect me to tell that to a rude fellow whom I meet in the street, even if he is cooling my brow for me with a fan?'

Assuming another voice, Alim said: 'Away, ruffian! Can't you see that the Khan wants to talk to *me* about his emeralds?'

But the Grand Khan was not to be drawn, and refused to say anything to Alim after that.

The next night Alim tried again. Sitting beside the Khan he said:

'Your emeralds have been stolen!'

'Don't talk nonsense!' said the Khan – but, since Alim did not say any more, the thought rolled backwards and forwards in his mind in his sleep. While Alim sat there silently, the Khan called out to the Khanum in the adjoining room, 'Malika, have you the emeralds safe?'

The Khanum answered:

'Yes of course, they are under my bed, as they have always been.'

So the Khan, muttering 'Stupid oaf!' slipped into a relieved and profound slumber once more.

Alim the Artful waited until the Khanum's breathing showed that she was deeply asleep and then he slipped into her room and took the emeralds.

That night he gave them to an honest man whom he had met in the serai, who had escaped from prison. This man slipped from the city before it was searched by the furious Khan's men, who practically demolished every house looking for the treasure.

The criers shouted the Royal proclamation in the street that 'Theft always leads to disgrace and destruction, and the emeralds must be returned forthwith.' Since the people were muttering against the Khan and all his works, nobody noticed anything unusual about Alim's saying whenever he heard the criers: 'Since theft has become the order of the day here, how can it be dishonourable?'

Now the Khan called the wisest man in all the land to advise him how to catch the thief, even if he could not get his emeralds back. 'We must make an example of him, otherwise he will become more and more audacious,' said the Khan. He added: 'You wisest men in all the land will, I am sure, provide a perfect trap. But just to hasten matters, I will have you put in a dungeon until you work one out.'

HOW ALIM PROVED THAT HE WAS A DOCTOR

The soldiers of the Khan, while this was going on, were searching the city for strangers, because the people had been intimidated for so long that it was the Khan's belief that the thief must be a foreigner of some kind. It was thus that they came upon Alim the Artful in his caravanserai and, unsatisfied by his claim that he was a doctor, carried him before the Grand Khan.

'Are you a doctor?' asked the Khan.

'Indeed I am, a special kind of doctor,' said Alim.

'Then you must cure someone at once, or we'll put you to the torture to see whether you are the thief,' said the Khan.

'Like all doctors, I have my rules,' said Alim, for he had hit upon a plan.

'Abide by your rules, so long as you do not decline to treat a patient,' said the Khan.

'My rule is that I should be allowed to select the patient.'

'You may certainly do so, providing that there is quite obviously something wrong with him,' said the Khan.

'Nothing easier,' said Alim. 'Do you see that blind man over there? I elect to cure him.'

'That would indeed prove that you were a very special kind of doctor,' said the Khan, 'for he is my son-in-law, and has been blind in both eyes for twenty years.'

'Get ready for the cure...' said Alim, advancing towards the patient.

'Your Highness,' murmured the Grand Vizier in alarm into the Khan's ear, 'don't forget that your daughter is so ugly that you had to find a blind man to marry her. Now, if his sight should be restored...'

'Enough!' shouted the Khan. 'Throw this man Alim out – he is no longer under suspicion.'

HOW ALIM MADE HIS FIRST DISCIPLE

Now Alim the Artful thought that he would lie low for a while, just in case the Khan had second thoughts about him, so he returned to his native glens.

In Kabul he was munching dried white mulberries and nuts, having spent his last penny, when he thought he would try to collect some capital.

He saw a man coming past the *chaikhana* where he was sitting, and called out to him: 'Friend, give me some money!'

'I haven't got any,' said the man.

'Well, give me something, a gift or even a piece of advice.'

'I haven't either.'

'What is your name?' asked Alim.

'I am called Chogh the Thin,' said the man.

'Chogh the Thin, you haven't much to lose. Would you like to become a disciple?'

'What is your Path?'

'The Artful Path. I am none other than Alim the Artful.'

'Well,' said Chogh the Thin, 'I hadn't heard of your *Tariqa* before, but it may be a secret and therefore a powerful one. I'll join you.'

So Chogh and Alim teamed up.

HOW ALIM TAUGHT CHOGH STORYTELLING

Chogh, who had a healthy appetite, said to Alim, 'Master, I am your disciple now, and here we are in this teahouse without the means to buy a cup of tea. I know that the pupil should help to feed the master, and I am ready to earn something. But what does one do when the disciple is hungry?'

'That is no problem,' said Alim, 'because when the disciple is hungry the master finds a way to feed him. It is not for the disciple to propose that he should earn something when he is manifestly incapable of doing so. It is almost impiety, and near to hypocrisy.'

And Alim addressed the other people in the teahouse, saying, in the first words that came into his head, 'Brothers, I could do with some chicken soup, I feel as much like it as a fox. Would you care to buy me some if I tell you how a sage changed the habits of a fox?'

Some of the people agreed, and Alim began:

THE STORY OF THE FOX AND THE CHICKENS

'Roba the Fox used to raid the henhouses of a certain village every night. He was so sly and so efficient that the villagers could never catch him. Soon he was supplying all the other foxes for miles around with chickens, for he found that he could not stop catching chickens.

'At last the villagers decided to call in the local sage to help. They said: "Great Sage, catch Roba the Fox for us, and stop him killing our chickens."

'The sage agreed. Using a special talisman which he had, he made the fox come to him. When the villagers saw that he had the fox, they cried, "Kill him, so that we shall not be worried any more by foxes."

'But the sage said: "I did not agree to kill the fox, only to stop him catching chickens."

'As they watched, the sage took off the dervish stone pendant emblem of his initiation, and hung it by a thong around the fox's neck. Then he let it go.

'The villagers said: "How can such a thing prevent chickens from being caught by a fox?"

'The sage replied: "Not only men, but all of creation, flee and conceal themselves from the truth. When the chickens, like mankind, glimpse this stone, they will hide themselves so well that even a fox will not be able to find them."

'And so it was. The fox, unable to catch any chickens after that, came to live with the sage, who shared his food with it, and used to call the fox, "Roba, my fellow dervish".'

With the money which they collected from the telling of this tale, Chogh and Alim were able to while away a few days in the Afghan capital, as well as eating their fill of chicken *pilau*.

'Come,' said Alim to Chogh, 'it is time we started on our travels again, for Kabul is hot and dusty. Has it not been said that "Artfulness is movement. An Artful man settled down becomes a deceitful man"?'

As they walked along the highway towards Jalalabad, they saw a strange-looking man coming towards them.

'Let us stop him,' said Alim, 'and see what cunning we can exercise upon this apparition.'

When they were within a few paces of the stranger, Alim said: 'May you never be tired, brother, what is your origin and what your destination, and what news do you bring?'

The man heaved a great sigh and said, in a halting manner:

'May you be safe! I come from a country a year's walk to the west, and I have come to sit at the feet of the Wise, for I have heard that the lands of the Persians and the Afghans are where the real wisdom of ancient times is still to be found.'

'Welcome, and welcome, and welcome,' said Alim. 'There is indeed ancient wisdom here, but unfortunately most of those who seek it look only at the obvious. Would you like me to show you some?'

The stranger, whose name was Yunus, accepted gratefully, and the three betook themselves to a caravanserai to discuss matters.

Yunus explained that he was looking for a teacher who would tell him and show him wonders and evidences of the secret wisdom of the ancients.

'It might cost you a great deal, in money and otherwise,' said Alim.

'I am prepared for any cost,' said Yunus, 'for I am a rich man, and have only adopted the dervish robe in order to appear more acceptable on the road.'

Yunus had heard of a great sage who had talking animals, and could make inanimate objects obey his will.

'Such things are plentiful, but they are in concealment,' said Alim, 'and you are lucky to have met us, for we will be able to shed some light upon the matter for you.'

The next morning Alim roused Chogh before dawn and said to him:

'Yunus is still asleep. Late last night I bought these twin goats from a merchant at this serai. You, as my disciple, must obey me in every particular, so make note of what I am saying. March ahead towards Jalalabad with one of these goats. At midday, halt and make tea. When we catch up with you, answer everything that I say with "Yes", unless I say "How did you know?", in which case you will answer "The goat told me."'

Chogh repeated his instructions, to make sure that he understood them.

'And,' added Alim, 'take this piece of stick and keep it in your pocket. Give it to me when I ask you about the meal.'

Later in the morning, Alim woke Yunus and said: 'We must be off, for I have affairs to attend to in Jalalabad.'

Alim unhitched the goat's lead from a post, said something into its ear and gave it a smack. The goat careered off down the road.

'What did you do?' asked Yunus.

'I was sending a message,' said Alim.

As they walked down the road, Alim took the twin brother of the stick which he had given Chogh and threw it into the air, saying: 'Stick, do your work.'

Towards midday, they came upon Chogh making a pot of tea by the roadside. Near him was tethered the twin goat.

Alim said: 'Did the goat bring you my message about saying your prayers in a certain form?'

'Yes,' said Chogh.

'How did you know to make the tea at this precise moment?'

'The goat told me,' said Chogh.

Yunus the traveller was transported with delight.

'A miracle! To think that I have blundered into companionship with people of the ancient wisdom!' he cried.

Alim looked at him. 'Are you satisfied with the evidence which you have received?' he asked.

'Yes, yes, more than satisfied,' said Yunus, 'and I beg you to accept me as a disciple, so that I may learn the wisdom.'

'You may ask me one question, on the basis of which I will decide your suitability for spiritual studies,' said Alim the Artful.

'Well, there is the matter of the stick. When we were on the road, you said that you were "sending a message" and you threw it into the air. What was that?'

'I was sending a message to Chogh about the feeding arrangements,' said Alim.

'But how?'

'By an inanimate object. Don't you remember that the wise have talking animals and can make inanimate objects obey their will? Show him the message-stick, Chogh.'

Chogh took the duplicate stick from his belt.

Yunus almost swooned with delight.

'Will you accept me? There is nothing that I want more in all the world,' he said.

'I am afraid that you have failed my test,' said Alim. 'But I can do more than accept you as a disciple: I can explain to you that you do not seek wisdom if you are attracted by trickery. The people whose reputations you are so impressed with are doing things which are incomprehensible to you and so you think they are miracles. Some, like us, are even charlatans.

'I studied for years under a Sufi master, and the first thing he taught me is what we are teaching you: "Have no preconceptions, and be humble". It is your arrogance which makes you think that you have found a Master.'

And that was how Yunus learned, when Alim explained the tricks, how to seek. He gave the two a handsome present and set off on his travels again.

HOW ALIM MET MOUR THE SLIGHT

When Alim and Chogh reached Jalalabad, they went to a caravanserai to hear the latest news and to refresh themselves. All the merchants there were agog because a spy had reported from Kabul that sacks of gold were being sent to their town for safe-keeping, since there had been so much thievery in the capital city.

'Ha!' said Alim. 'It is just as well that we set out in advance, otherwise they would be searching the city for strangers, in case thieves come after the gold.'

There had not been a theft in Jalalabad for decades, as the Khan there was peculiarly harsh with thieves of all kinds.

'Nobody dares to steal anything here,' said Chogh, when he returned from a gossip-collecting expedition in the bazaars, 'because the Khan is so very fierce.'

'What is the Khan like?' asked Alim.

'The Khans here are usually good, but this one is terrible,' said Chogh.

'Very well,' said Alim, 'we shall teach him a lesson.'

That very night Chogh and Alim lingered near the citadel, waiting for the consignment of gold. Sure enough, it arrived, in heavy bags on bullock-carts. In order to show the soldiers from Kabul escorting the consignment that Jalalabad was safe and honest, there was just one man with a cudgel waiting to receive it.

The Kabuli troops withdrew after getting a receipt, and Alim and Chogh walked up to the man with the cudgel.

'May you never be tired!' said Alim.

'May your shadow never grow less,' replied the man.

'What is your name?' asked Alim.

'They call me Mour the Slight,' said the man, who was a towering giant with much muscle and little brain, 'but sometimes I am called

Three-brains, because the walnut is called "four brains" in our language.'

'Do you know who I am?' asked Alim.

'No, Agha,' said Mour.

'That's very fortunate. I must see that everyone is rewarded for keeping the secret so well,' said Alim.

'What secret?' asked Mour, scratching his head in puzzlement.

'That I am from the Highest Authority,' said Alim.

'Not the Captain of the Guard?' asked Mour, who had hardly heard of anyone more important.

'There is someone more significant even than the Captain of the Guard,' said Alim, 'and I am his immediate representative. The Captain of the Guard, compared with me, is like the mouse compared with the elephant.'

Mour was most impressed. Anyone who could speak like that about the Captain of the Guard must be a man of consequence.

'Well, as the saying has it, "first the food and then the speech",' said Alim, 'and so you'd better go and get the bullock-carts, and tell the people who have them that it is very important that they be here soon and if they are, we might consider hiring more of them for secret affairs like this.'

'Shall I go to the Khanly Stables?' asked Mour.

'No, you fool! This is a secret matter. Thieves might have their spies there. Go and get bullocks from someone who has never supplied them to the Khan before.'

So, in not much more time that it takes to tell, Mour went to a bullock-cart hiring stables and brought back two carts. Mour had given him, as a deposit, all the remaining money from Yunus's gift. It was so much that the owner of the carts hoped that they would never be returned, so that he could take the huge deposit instead.

At that moment a soldier of the Khan came up, and asked why the three were so busy loading bags of gold onto a bullock-cart.

'Knock him out with your cudgel,' said Alim to Mour.

'Why?' asked Mour. 'For surely he is on our side?'

'You yokels are all the same,' said Alim. 'Do as I say and I will tell you afterwards.'

Mour knocked the soldier senseless, and Alim the Artful trussed him up while the others got the rest of the gold into the carts.

When all was ready they started to move out of town. Alim said: 'I told you that I would explain why you had to knock out the soldier, and I will, for I am a man of my word. Didn't you notice that he spoke with a slight accent? That was the Paghman way of talking. Now, in our valleys we are so tough that we have a special form of endearment which is reserved only for our fellow Paghmanis. This is to knock each other out in friendliness, just as you more effete people clap a friend on the shoulder. I asked you to do it because I was busy loading the gold. It is what we call the "Paghman Salaam".'

'You must be men indeed, you men of the mountains,' said Mour, 'and it must be for this reason that they have the saying: "Curse the strongest man in the world, but do not say as much as 'Good Morning' to a Paghmani."'

Presently they reached a field where they buried the gold. They found a Kochi nomad encampment, where Alim was received like a lost brother. Alim said: 'Brothers, tonight we feast!' And he presented the bullocks to the Kochis, who tore them into strips in what seemed like a few seconds, and roasted the pieces over a fire. The Kochis told everyone's fortunes, and then Alim said: 'Friends, if anyone comes looking for bullocks, I am sure that none of us will have heard of any.'

The Inward Observer

ROBA THE FOX really admired himself, and was convinced that all his opinions were true facts – opinions, after all, were what lesser beings had, not Roba.

One day as he was thinking this, some chickens came pecking their way along the road. As soon as they saw him they fled, fluttering and clucking for all they were worth.

Roba ran after them and when they were winded and cowering, he asked them what they were doing. 'We are running away because we are frightened of you – you might eat us!'

'It is only your opinion. I am sure that it is a fact that I have no aggression in me, and that I would not eat you,' answered Roba. 'But, in order to teach you, rather than to test myself, let us demonstrate. You chickens just try your best to incense me.'

So the chickens, their curiosity aroused, pecked at him and scuffed up stones at him, while they laughed louder and louder as he did not react at all.

Suddenly the fox snarled and, as the fowls streaked away in alarm, he shouted: 'Now I know why foxes chase chickens. If they did not, and everyone behaved like you, fox life would be intolerable. It only appears to the outward observer that a fox always makes the first aggressive move.'

Latif and the Miser's Gold

THERE WAS ONCE a miser who was so extremely mean that when he had to go away for a time and wanted someone to watch his bags of gold he could not find anyone to do it except a woman who was so stupid that she believed him when he said he would pay her for the service.

Latif the Thief heard something about this. He walked straight into the miser's house and picked up the bags of gold.

The woman was sitting there, watching the gold, and when she saw him she said:

'Who do you think you are, taking that gold away?'

Latif said:

'I am Latif the Thief, if it's any business of yours!'

The woman said:

'I may be stupid, but you are the stupidest man I ever heard of! Not only do you walk in here in broad daylight and pick up the miser's entire fortune, but you even tell me your name!'

Latif had worked it all out in advance. He said:

'You wouldn't give Latif the Thief away, would you, just because he took a little gold?'

The woman said:

'You can't get round me like that, you know. I know my duty, and I'll testify in court against you.'

'Madam, you do just that,' said Latif; 'and to repay evil with good, I'll tell you how to avoid going blind!'

She said:

'What do you mean, go blind?'

'Don't you see the blinding rain outside?' asked Latif. 'Well, if you don't hold your hands over your eyes and count thirty, you'll go blind. You have heard the phrase "blinding rain", haven't you? Now we have that phrase because of the real, original, blinding rain, which doesn't often fall. I'm an expert, and I can tell you that this is the real, the original, blinding rain that is falling now. It doesn't often happen; but as a thief I'm out in all weathers and have to know about things like that.'

The stupid woman said:

'Thank you indeed! I'm grateful to you, don't think I am not, but duty is duty, and I shall have to report what happened and who did it.'

She covered her eyes with her hands, though, and counted thirty as Latif bore the gold away.

When the miser came home he was furious, both that the gold was gone and because Latif had walked in and taken it in broad daylight. He called the police and they soon tracked down and arrested Latif the Thief who had meanwhile very carefully concealed the gold so that it was not to be found.

Latif was taken to court and the woman testified; and when it was his turn to speak, he said to the judge:

'Your Honour, in the first place this woman says that I went into the house and told her my name and stole the gold. Now, what self-respecting thief would do that? Secondly I would like to ask her a question.'

The judge said: 'Very well, ask her.'

Latif said: 'Madam, when was it that I stole the gold?'

And she said: 'Well, don't you remember? It was the evening of the blinding rain.'

Latif said: 'Would you mind telling the court what the blinding rain is, because they might not know.'

'Certainly,' said the woman, 'it is the rain that our blinding rain is named after. It is the rain that actually *does* make you blind and unless you hold your hands over your eyes and count thirty you will be struck blind.'

Latif said to the judge: 'Your Honour, as I have just shown, this is hardly a reliable witness; I submit that she never saw me steal anything any more than she ever endured any blinding rain.'

And he won the case.

Now, everyone has heard of the people who say that because a person is unreliable in one thing, he must be unreliable in everything. Well, believe it or not, this is the original case on which this very logical idea is based. Latif the Thief thus takes his place in history as a person who has contributed something to human civilisation.

He taught us that if a person says one thing unreliable then everything which he does is likely to be unreliable. And we all know that that's true – don't we?

Of course nowadays in real life the general level of cultural anticipation of events has improved. Nobody entrusts responsibility to people too stupid to discharge it properly: any more than they teach people things which they are not yet ready to understand. But the case of the gold? I am afraid that through some lack of co-ordination of facts, it is still on the files as unsolved.

When Dishonest is Honest

ALIM, AN OLD friend, went one day with Latif on a journey. They travelled fast, and after several days they arrived at a village where Latif was received with great respect by the people.

'People are waiting for you, Latif Baba,' they said.

Latif and Alim were taken to a house where Latif at once sat down and started to see the large number of people who had been waiting, some for months, until he arrived.

He saw them one by one.

Alim watched while Latif listened to what each person wanted. Some of them needed money, others work, others were artists, some were people who wanted to promote some kind of new idea, some were looking for special doctors who could treat difficult cases.

To each and every one of them Latif gave a letter, addressed to some prince, noble, specialist, artisan, king or merchant, or to an official, or the mayor of a town, or to a mullah, or to some other person, important or otherwise.

When Latif had seen all the people, over a week had passed.

Then the villagers came and said:

'Great Latif Baba: the gifts await you.'

Latif and Alim were taken to a warehouse, which was full of every kind of commodity. There were silks and satins, robes of honour, bags of gold, sacks of rare and interesting items. There were plates of gold and hand-worked scarves; curiosities and foodstuffs, dried fruits and jewels, sweetmeats and arms, bowls of cut crystal – almost everything one could imagine, large and small, valuable and insignificant.

Latif called upon the people who were waiting for the warehouse to be opened, and asked them their business, one by one. As each person left, Latif assigned him a gift from the warehouse, until nothing was left.

This all took up a further week.

When that was finished, Latif said to Alim:

'Come, we shall return to our other life.'

When they were on the road again, Alim said to Latif:

'Good Latif, what was the meaning of what we have been through during the past fortnight, for I cannot understand it however much I try.'

Latif laughed. 'How could you understand something, and why should you try, if you do not know what went before?'

Alim asked Latif to tell him why and how he came to be in the position of a baba, a sort of saint.

Latif said:

'Many years ago, when I was a disciple of a great man, he ordered me to travel to every country in the world. While I was there, I was to familiarise myself with the customs and problems and the people of importance and their needs, and the peculiarities of each region.

'This exercise occupied me for seven years. When it was over, I was able to make use of the vast store of knowledge which I had accumulated. Let me illustrate:

'Take the man who had invented a new kind of chair for people with one leg. Now, during my travels I was in the land of the one-legged people. Hardly anyone else knows about it. But they are the people to buy the chair, and to make that inventor happy and rich until the end of his days. So all I had to do was to tell him how to get there. And the same with the people who wanted donkeys, or healing, or who needed education, or who realised that they were in the wrong position. Like a guide at a crossroads, I was able to point out the way.'

'And what was the meaning of the things in the warehouse?' asked Alim.

'Quite simple. When people gained what they wanted in following my instructions, they naturally sent me something to give out to the less fortunate, and that was what I was doing during the second week of our stay at the village.'

Alim was amazed, for he realised that he knew hardly anything about the extraordinary Latif, while he had imagined that he knew all about him.

'But why not settle down and become a holy man, a baba?' he said. 'In that way you would not have to be a thief.'

'Do I really have to remind you again,' said Latif, 'that I am a thief because the ordinary men of the world consider themselves to be honest, and not because they are honest or I am dishonest. A dishonest baba, claiming respect because he knows where to get things or where to send people, is more of a thief than the man who takes what has been stolen in the first place and restores it to its rightful owner.'

Unbalanced

NASRUDIN WAS A master of the answer which corresponds to the mentality or the intentions of the speaker.

Once, someone taking him for an idiot asked:

'Why do some people walk in one direction and others in the opposite direction?'

Nasrudin at once said:

'Well, if they all walked on the same part of the earth, it would become overweighted and turn upside down.'

True Story

AN ENGLISH SEEKER after Truth once sold everything he had and wandered to the East, where he spent all his time looking for a suitable Sufi teacher, convinced that this was what he must do.

After eight years of this life, he came upon a dervish, and asked him if he knew the way to arrive at the door of the Teacher of the Age.

'Certainly,' said the dervish. He immediately wrote down a name and address.

The Englishman was naturally most impressed and grateful, and for a moment he could hardly believe that his quest was almost ended. Then he looked at the paper, and said:

'But this is someone who lives in London. And his house is not five minutes' walk from my old home!'

'Exactly,' said the dervish; 'and that is not all. If you had stayed where you were, and made reasonable enquiries instead of arrogant and flamboyant gestures like wandering over the earth without permission – you would have met him six years ago.'

The Murder

ONE DAY, OVER a thousand years ago, a number of building labourers were carrying sacks up ladders during the construction of a house. One of them seemed to be in an unusually good humour. Nobody would have imagined that there was anything especially undesirable about him.

But the Abbasi Caliph Al-Mutadid, looking at the scene from his window, became curious about this labourer. He had enquiries made as to whether the man was drunk or mad, or whether there was any special reason for his elation.

When it was reported to the Caliph that nothing unusual was known about the man, he was immediately called to the imperial presence.

The Caliph ordered him to be beaten, and asked how much money he had.

After a short time, the labourer admitted that he possessed a thousand gold pieces. When he was further asked how he got it, he confessed.

'In the evenings I work as a stoker at a Turkish bath,' he said, 'and recently a man ran in and asked me to look after him. He had been drinking. I covered him with some rubbish in a corner.

'Soon afterwards some other drunks ran in after him, but I told them that he was not there, and they left. When I went back to him he had lost consciousness. I searched him and found a thousand gold pieces on him.

'I stole this money and disposed of the man by burning him in the furnace.'

The Caliph had an investigation made and it was discovered that the man was a foreigner. The Caliph had the money given to trustees to be transmitted to the murdered man's family.

In accordance with custom, the stoker was himself burnt in a furnace for his crime.

This was one of the occasions when Caliphial perception caused an example which prevented people from committing crimes for years on end. Potential criminals were terrified that they might be discovered by some sort of supernatural prescience which their ruler seemed to have.

When he was asked by a few intimates as to how he had arrived at the conclusion that something was amiss with the murderer, Al-Mutadid said:

'This man's behaviour did not accord with his temperament, his work or his condition. Knowing the type I realised that in some way he had become possessed of money.'

A Request

If you enjoyed this book, please review it on Amazon and Goodreads.

Reviews are an author's best friend.

To stay in touch with news on forthcoming editions of Idries Shah works, please sign up for the mailing list:

 http://bit.ly/ISFlist

And to follow him on social media, please go to any of the following links:

 https://twitter.com/idriesshah

 https://www.facebook.com/IdriesShah

 http://www.youtube.com/idriesshah999

 http://www.pinterest.com/idriesshah/

 http://bit.ly/ISgoodreads

 http://idriesshah.tumblr.com

 https://www.instagram.com/idriesshah/

http://idriesshahfoundation.org